MW01078281

No Dig
Cookbook

© Charles Dowding 2022

Published by No Dig Garden 2022 Imprint of Charles Dowding Ltd

Edited by Anna Maskell
Proofread by Elisabeth Ingles
Indexed by Jo Penning

Designed by James Pople

Photography by James Pople, Charles Dowding,
Edward Dowding, Lucy Pope, Briony Plant

ISBN: 978-1-9160920-7-5

Printed by Cambrian Press Ltd, The Pensord Group, Tram Road,
Pontllanfraith, Blackwood, NP12 2YA

Distributed by CBL Distribution, Cambrai Court, 1229 Stratford Road,
Hall Green, Birmingham, B28 9AA. 01216 083950

No Dig Cookbook

Seasonal feasts from
homegrown vegetables

CATHERINE BALAAM
& CHARLES DOWDING

Contents

Foreword

Charles Dowding

It has been a pleasure to work with Catherine on this project. She is a gardener too, therefore appreciates the values of homegrown vegetables, and how to make them vibrant in many ways.

From your garden, you can exult in aromas, flavours and health-giving qualities of freshly picked produce. This book is to help you celebrate them in a tasty and beautiful way.

The no dig approach to growing makes it more likely that you grow successfully. It's a simple process which anybody can succeed with. The two tenets are:

1. Leave soil undisturbed.
2. Feed soil life with organic matter on the surface.

Then it's a question of how to succeed with each vegetable, and I share many of my best tips for growing them.

Combine your harvests with nice methods in the kitchen, such as Catherine describes, and you have a feast. A super healthy one too, thanks to invisible soil microbes on the vegetables, often the same as those needed by our guts for healthy digestion.

The flavour spectrum of vegetables grown in healthy soil often surpasses those of store-bought food. Hence the simple ease of these recipes, without long lists of extra ingredients: a rich-tasting dish is not difficult to achieve.

Plus we offer ideas for extending the season of eating, beyond any season's final harvest of that vegetable. Catherine explains methods for pickling and fermenting, while I offer tips on storing the vegetables.

Introduction

Catherine Balaam

I didn't realise it at the time, but I was lucky when I was growing up. My dad grew almost all of our veg and my mum was a cook by profession, well-known and celebrated for her food in the local area. As the vegetables that Dad grew were lovingly transformed into delicious meals, we always ate very well as a family. Because of this privilege (and I do very much count it as a privilege), I've always loved food. When I was younger that love was focused on eating, but as I got older I realised that if you want to enjoy good food then you need to learn to make it yourself. I also realised that nothing ever tastes as good as something you've nurtured and grown in your own garden. Finally, about ten years ago, I took on an allotment and slowly began to move towards growing all the fruit and veg that I eat now.

I've been following Charles and his methods for about eight years, since being inspired by one of his talks. His passion was infectious, and once I started doing 'no dig' I saw that it was the way forward for me. My dad had been supplying me with seedlings and when I started the no dig method we both noticed my plants were healthier and bigger than his. After going on a day course with Charles at Homeacres, Dad switched to the no dig method too. This, combined with his decades of experience, now makes his allotment the envy of all in his growing community. I've taken the example of my parents and explored further, diving into the world of fermenting as a way of preserving those big gluts of veg. As well as keeping me through the winter months, this improves nutritional benefit and revitalises gut health with the probiotics that fermentation creates.

My work has always been in the field of health and wellbeing, and I've always felt that growing food and eating well is such an important part of good health. Not just physically, but also emotionally. When I was offered the opportunity to work with Charles and cook for his courses, it was a dream come true. I love cooking and preserving food and Charles is my gardening hero. This wasn't just about feeding hungry customers on demand, but celebrating the amazing results of growing in a way that nourishes the earth as well as us.

I'm not a trained chef but an enthusiastic eater. In my world there's little better than eating great-tasting fresh vegetables prepared with love. I don't have time to spend hours in the kitchen every day, but I do want to enjoy my food and feel that I'm supporting my health. I think that's possible with good quality veg and a few simple recipes like those you'll find here. So I hope this book inspires you to explore culinary adventures with the vegetables you produce, using the useful hints and tips from Charles on how to get the best results from your garden.

These recipes are all easy to achieve for anyone, no matter what your cooking ability. Each recipe should only take between 5 and 30 minutes to prepare, plus any cooking time for beans, roasties and stews. This doesn't include podding of beans and peas, which is an unavoidably time-consuming task (rope someone else in to help with this when you can). Please read the 'Eat what you've grown' sections so you can adapt the recipes to use what you have available. Combine side dishes to make a vegetarian feast full of flavour. Be adventurous, and try altering the recipes to suit your harvests beyond what I have suggested. This book is offered as a guideline to encourage you to enjoy your produce in new ways.

No knead bread

Charles Dowding

Use this simple method for all types of bread, whether made with yeast or a sourdough starter.

The grain can be wheat or rye, whole or refined. My preference is very much for wholegrain, and for top nutritional quality I make bread from freshly ground flour, using a small stone mill I purchased in 1983. Fresh-milled flour contains vitamin E and oils which start to decompose straight after milling. Hence bakers find it easier to use white flour, a less lively and more stable product.

To make a starter, mix wholegrain flour with lukewarm water, to a runny consistency. Leave in a jar open to air, in the warmest place of your house. Within a few days you notice bubbles at the surface, as wild yeasts arrive and start to ferment the starch. After 5–7 days, use this fermenting mix as a starter for your first batch of bread.

1. A few hours before mixing into the main batch of dough, multiply your starter's yeasts. Add 100–150g / 3–5oz flour and enough warm water to have a sloppy mix, a batter more than a dough at this stage. In winter, keep this warm so that the yeasts multiply fast.

Makes 2 x 830g / 1lb 13oz loaves

1kg / 2lb 3oz flour
750ml / 3 cups water
1–2 tbsp oil
I don't add salt but you
   can if you want

2. Add the fermenting, bubbly batter to all the flour, with enough lukewarm water to make a mix that is just possible to stir with a spoon. Put a spoonful of the new dough back into your starter pot, with a lid on. Keep in a fridge until you next bake, with no intermediate attention or feeding, for up to a month or more! The yeasts stay quite dormant at low temperatures.

3. You can add salt to taste (I add none) and a little oil, say 1 or 2 tablespoons per half kilo of flour. This gives a smooth textured dough, and ensures a clean cut when you slice the bread.

4. Oil tins or trays, spoon the dough into or onto them, and use a knife to level. Lay a piece of plastic over the top to conserve moisture and enable a slow rise, without a crust forming.

5. 6–8 hours later, the dough will be 50% higher, and ready to bake at 180°C / 350°F for around an hour.

6. Remove the loaves and leave to cool. If you eat them within a few hours, you will consume twice the amount compared to eating on subsequent days!

7. The consistency is moister than kneaded bread. It keeps well for at least five days, at ambient temperature. The ease of making it allows anybody to achieve and enjoy homemade bread, without any machine.

See my video on YouTube, 'Seed to Threshing to Milling to No Knead Bread'.

Pestos, dips and sauces

Aioli

Tahini dressing

Carrot top pesto

Dried tomato pesto

Nettle and mint pesto

Beetroot hummus

Dried tomato hummus

Borlotti bean hummus

Roasted red pepper hummus

Carrot and parsnip dip

Aioli

Aioli

I use this as a base for quite a few salads, some of which you'll find in this book. It is so quick and easy, and tastes way better than adding shop-bought mayonnaise to your dishes. At Homeacres we like it pretty garlicky, but of course you can use less garlic if you prefer.

1. Add the garlic, mustard and egg yolks to a blender and blitz into a paste. Then, very slowly to start with, add your olive oil. Check to see if your blender is mixing properly. I find that as it is such a small mix to begin with, anything that is under the blade doesn't mix in and I have to stop and get in there with a spatula a couple of times until there is a bit more mass. If you add your oil too quickly in the beginning, your aioli will not emulsify, so go carefully until you see it start to thicken. Once it is thickening, you can then add the rest of the oil more quickly.

2. Once all the oil is added, add your lemon juice and give it a final mix before popping it into a bowl to serve.

You can store aioli in an airtight container in the fridge for up to 4–5 days.

Serves 6–8

3 cloves of garlic, minced
2 egg yolks
1 tbsp Dijon mustard
400ml / 1¾ cups of extra virgin olive oil (if you prefer your aioli less rich, then use half extra virgin olive oil and half light olive oil)
juice of ½ lemon

Tahini dressing

This dressing goes with almost anything. I drizzle it over roast veggies, I love it slathered over steamed veg and rice, and the runnier version makes a great salad dressing. I think it tastes better if you use fermented garlic (see p.53), but before I started fermenting I made it for years with raw garlic. It was always great.

1. Add all ingredients to a jar, seal and shake well to mix. Make sure there are no lumps of tahini. If there are, squish them with the back of a teaspoon and then shake your jar again.

If you want a runnier dressing then add a tablespoon of slightly warm water.

Serves 6–8

1 tbsp tahini
1 tsp tamari
1 tbsp lemon juice
3 tbsp olive oil
2 cloves of garlic, crushed

Tahini dressing with roasted Crown Prince squash

Pesto

Here are a few of my favourite pesto recipes. Unlike traditional pesto recipes, you will notice that I always use yeast flakes instead of parmesan and sunflower seeds instead of pine nuts.

My reason for using yeast flakes is that parmesan is quite strong and I prefer something a little more subtle to let the flavour of the main ingredient really be the star of the show. Yeast flakes still have a cheesy taste but without being overbearing.

Plus, without the cheese it is then a vegan dish, which makes it more accessible for everyone, a key factor when cooking for the no dig courses.

If you want to replace the yeast flakes with parmesan then feel free to give it a go and see which you prefer.

I use sunflower seeds as this is just the taste that I like. You can use cashews, walnuts or pine nuts instead, or a combination of any of these, so use whatever you have in the cupboard and experiment with the different flavours that the other nuts offer.

These recipes will give you quite a thick finished product. I make them like this so I can spread on crackers or toast, and if I want to use them as more of a sauce for pasta then I just add more olive oil.

I encourage you to be brave and experiment finding the flavours and consistency that you prefer. We all have slightly different tastes and these recipes are just a guideline to inspire you.

The amounts made differ, depending on the recipe. It is hard for me to estimate how many they will feed as I use these pestos in so many different ways. I like to use them lavishly while I know that some of you may prefer to be a little more conservative with strong flavours. To keep for some months in the fridge, put into sterilised jars with a layer of olive oil on top. This is to stop the sauce from coming into contact with oxygen, which is what causes mould. I stock my fridge with several different pestos in the summer to keep me going through the winter. They will also freeze really well if that is your preferred method of storage.

Opposite: Carrot top pesto

Carrot top pesto

There is no need to discard all those beautiful carrot tops, even if it is to feed your compost!

This is always such a popular dish in a Homeacres lunch, I think mostly because people think it will taste earthy and bitter, and then they are pleasantly surprised by the fresh flavour.

It is a bright and tasty pesto that you can make whatever time of year you are pulling your carrots, if the tops are still fresh. I particularly love the fact that no part of a carrot is wasted, because when you are growing your own every bit is so valuable.

1. Sort the carrot tops and get rid of the thick stems and anything that is yellowing.
2. Place all carrot tops and the remaining ingredients in a blender and blend until smooth. You can add a little more oil if you would like a runnier pesto.

large bunch of carrot tops
4 cloves of garlic, peeled and roughly chopped
100g / 3.5 oz sunflower seeds, lightly toasted
juice of 1 lemon
40g / 1.4oz of yeast flakes
100ml / ½ cup olive oil

Use what you've grown
You can add some parsley to this if you have it. I personally prefer to make a smaller batch and keep it as pure carrot tops as I love the flavour so much, but experiment and see what you prefer.

Rocket pesto

A great way to use lots of this peppery leaf when your rocket patch explodes. I think it is better with wild rocket than salad rocket as wild rocket has a bit more of a punch, but either is good.

1. Place all the ingredients in a blender and blend until well mixed but not quite smooth. You can add a little more oil if you would like a runnier pesto.

200g / 7oz rocket
4 cloves of garlic, peeled and roughly chopped
100g / 3.5oz of sunflower seeds, lightly toasted
juice of 1 lemon
35g / 1.2oz yeast flakes
4 tbsp olive oil

Use what you've grown
You can also add some parsley or a little mint to this pesto if you have it. It can soften the flavour a little when it's later in the season and your rocket is beginning to flower and is very strong and peppery.

Dried tomato pesto

This pesto is such a treat, and is really only if you have had a major glut of tomatoes the year before and have managed to dehydrate them (see p.87). It takes 10kg / 22lb of tomatoes to make 500g / 1lb 2oz of dried tomatoes, so there would be about 1.2kg / 2lb 10oz of fresh tomatoes in this recipe. Plant more tomatoes if you can!

I make sure I grow extra tomatoes so that I have enough to dry out in excess to make things like this. In my world, you can never have too many tomatoes. There's so much you can do with them, and drying (or fermenting, see p.52) means you can have that summery flavour in your food through the winter too.

If you use oven-roasted rather than fully dried tomatoes, they don't need rehydrating for a recipe like this. But triple the weight of tomatoes used.

1. Rehydrate your tomatoes by squishing into a small jug or bowl and only just covering with boiling water. Leave them for 10–15 minutes. You may want to weigh them down with a clean jar.

2. Drain the tomatoes and let them cool a little. Place all the ingredients in a blender and blend until smooth, along with some of the water you used to rehydrate the tomatoes. You can add a little more oil or tomato water if you would like a runnier pesto.

60g / 2oz dried tomatoes
2 cloves of garlic, peeled and
  roughly chopped
60g / 2oz sunflower seeds,
  lightly toasted
juice of ½ lemon
15g / 0.5oz yeast flakes
4 tbsp olive oil

Use what you've grown

You can replace 10g (or more) of tomatoes with the same amount of rocket to this pesto if you have it. It changes the flavour, but bulks it up if you don't have a lot of dried tomatoes.

Nettle and mint pesto

This is a great pesto and quite possibly my favourite thing to have in the fridge throughout the summer.

Pick just the top 4–6 leaves of young nettles. When picking, wear gloves, unless of course you don't mind being stung. Spring nettle sting is much more gentle than that of the big nettles later in the year, but it is still a sting. I always wear gloves as I pick so many.

Think about where you are collecting your nettles from. If it is along the edges of well-used dog walking routes they will probably have been peed on quite a bit, so maybe find a less accessible spot. I collect mine from the hedges around my allotment site, and I have now started cultivating a nettle area in my allotment so they are easily accessible. I can keep young nettles coming for a large part of the year by cropping them back to the ground once they get too big to pick, constantly encouraging new growth.

4 large handfuls of nettle tops
large bunch of mint
55g / 2oz sunflower seeds,
    lightly toasted
juice of ½ lemon
15g / 0.5oz of yeast flakes
2 tbsp olive oil

1. Prepare your nettle tops by going through them (with your gloves on) and making sure there are no large stems or little living creatures. Pop them in a pan of boiling water for a minute or two then drain (you can keep the water and drink it as nettle tea, which has multiple health benefits). Squeeze as much of the water out of them as you can.

2. Strip the mint leaves from the stems and place in a blender with the nettles and the remaining ingredients, then blitz until well mixed but not completely smooth. You can add more olive oil if you would like a runnier pesto. I like mine quite stiff, which is better for spreading on toast or crackers. If you want to use it on pasta then just add more olive oil.

I love this pesto spread on some toasted sourdough (or Charles's rye bread), with a slice of fresh tomato and a little salt and pepper on top. It's my absolute favourite snack!

Spicy Spanish potatoes with aioli; beetroot, squash and feta salad; dried tomato pesto

Hummus

You will notice that in all my hummus recipes I always use some of the water from the chickpeas, also known as aquafaba. This is often used as a vegan substitute for eggs as it whips and foams really nicely, which makes your hummus really creamy. If you use tinned chickpeas, then the water from the can is aquafaba, or if you cook your own, it's the water you've cooked them in.

If you have grown and dried Czar beans then you can use them instead of chickpeas in any of the hummus recipes, giving you a white bean hummus which is lighter and creamier than one made from chickpeas. The Czar bean water won't have the same effect so just use normal water, but you won't need very much so add it slowly.

All the hummus recipes will make you a good-sized bowlful that will be ideal to share with friends. What you don't use will keep in your fridge for about a week. It also freezes really well. When I make a batch that is not for a gathering, I keep a tub in the fridge and pop the rest in the freezer.

Opposite: Beetroot hummus

Beetroot hummus

This hummus always looks so bright and colourful on the table and it tastes great too. Serve it up surrounded by cucumber and celery sticks (if they're available) and really make that bright pink colour pop.

1. Heat the oven to 190°C / 375°F fan. Chop your beet into roughly 3cm / 1in chunks, toss in 1 tbsp of the oil and season lightly, then pop in the oven for about 25 minutes. You want it lightly cooked but not crispy.

2. Once the beetroot has cooled, place it in a blender with all the other ingredients, apart from the aquafaba, and blend together. Then add the aquafaba a little at a time until you get the consistency that you want, and continue to blend for a good minute or two. This will make your hummus really light and fluffy.

200g / 7oz beetroot
4 tbsp olive oil
250g / 9oz chickpeas (this is about one drained can); save the water from the can / cooking
2–4 cloves of garlic, depending on how much you like garlic
juice of 1½ lemons
2 tbsp tahini
½ tsp good quality salt
100ml / ½ cup chickpea water (aquafaba)
pepper to taste

Use what you've grown

Instead of the beetroot you could use any kind of squash. For this, toast one teaspoon each of cumin and coriander seeds, grind in a mortar and pestle, and then add to the tablespoon of oil that you use to coat your veg for roasting. Follow the rest of the recipe as above.

Dried tomato hummus

Charles dehydrates a lot of tomatoes during the summer so I am lucky to be able to make this. I don't have enough room in my kitchen for a dehydrator so I oven dry my extra tomatoes. If you don't have your own dried tomatoes then you can make this with store-bought sun-dried tomatoes.

1. Put your tomatoes in a small bowl or jug and only just cover them with boiling water, then leave for about 15 minutes or so to soften up. You may want to use a jar or something similar to weigh them down. If you are using store-bought sun-dried tomatoes, you may want to leave them longer to rehydrate (I suggest up to an hour). You want them to be soft to make this dish.

2. Once they are rehydrated, roughly chop your tomatoes and let them and the tomato water cool.

3. Place the tomatoes and their water in a blender with all the other ingredients, apart from the aquafaba, and blend until well mixed. Add the aquafaba a little at a time until you get the consistency that you want, and then blend for another good minute or two to get a nice, fluffy hummus.

40g / 1.4oz dried tomatoes
4 tbsp olive oil
250g / 9oz chickpeas (this is about one drained can); save the water from the can / cooking
2 cloves of garlic, crushed
juice of 1 lemon
2 tbsp tahini
1 tsp ground cumin
¼ tsp smoked paprika
¼ tsp good quality salt, can add more to taste
60ml / ¼ cup chickpea water (aquafaba)
pepper to taste

Borlotti bean hummus

This is a much deeper flavoured hummus than when using just chickpeas on their own. You can use only borlotti beans if you wish. This would be more of a strong flavour but still nice. I prefer to keep it a bit lighter by combining them with chickpeas.

1. Place all ingredients, apart from the aquafaba, in a blender and blend until well mixed. Add the aquafaba a little at a time until you get the consistency that you want, and then blend for a good minute or two to get your hummus nice and creamy.

250g / 9oz chickpeas (this is about one drained can); save the water from the can / cooking
250g / 9oz cooked borlotti beans (see p.40)
6 tbsp olive oil
3 cloves of garlic
juice from 1 ½ lemons
2 tbsp tahini
1 tsp ground cumin
½ tsp smoked paprika
¼ tsp good quality salt, can add more to taste
120ml / ½ cup chickpea water (aquafaba)
pepper to taste

Use what you've grown

If you have grown and dried Czar runner beans (once dried, Czar beans are much like butter beans), then you can always use these instead of chickpeas. This will make a creamier finished product.

Roasted red pepper hummus

Give your simple chickpea hummus a slightly smoky and sweet twist by simply adding roasted red pepper and a little smoked paprika. The roasting of the pepper intensifies the natural sweetness. This is a tasty variation during the summer months if you have red peppers to spare.

1. Remove the stalk and seeds and cut your peppers in half lengthways, then flatten them out as best you can. Place them under a hot grill, skin-side facing up, and cook until the skin has blistered and charred.

2. Pop them in a bowl and cover with a plate, then let them cool and sweat for 15 minutes. Once they are cool enough to handle, peel the skins off and chop the flesh.

2 red peppers
4 tbsp olive oil
250g / 9oz chickpeas (this is about one drained can); save the water from the can / cooking
2 cloves of garlic
juice of 1 lemon
2 tbsp tahini

Continued on next page

3. Place the peppers in a blender with all the other ingredients, apart from the aquafaba, and blend until well mixed. Add the aquafaba a little at a time until you get the consistency that you want, and then blend for another minute to get that nice smooth and fluffy texture.

½ tsp ground cumin
½ tsp smoked paprika
¼ tsp cayenne pepper
¼ tsp good quality salt, can add more to taste
60ml / ¼ cup chickpea water (aquafaba)
pepper to taste

Carrot and parsnip dip

This sounds like an odd combination but trust me, it works really well. The sweetness of the carrots and parsnips comes out when roasted, and the orange really lifts the flavour of these winter roots.

1. Heat your oven to 190°C / 375°F fan. Roast the cumin, coriander and caraway seeds in a dry frying pan until the aromas of the spices are released. Then grind in a mortar and pestle to a rough powder.

2. Peel the parsnips and chop them and the carrots into large chunks. There is no need to peel your carrots if they are homegrown and / or organic, and if you are using baby parsnips then there is no need to peel them either. Mix the ground spices with 60ml / ¼ cup of the olive oil, then toss the veg in the spicy oil until nicely coated and spread onto a baking tray. Roast in the oven for around half an hour, or until your veg is cooked through but not crispy.

3. When the veg has cooled, put into a blender with all the other ingredients and mix until smooth. If it is too thick then add a little water until you get the consistency you like. Add salt and pepper to taste.

1 tsp cumin seeds
1 tsp coriander seeds
½ tsp caraway seeds
120ml / ½ cup olive oil
250g / 9oz carrots, any colour
200g / 7oz parsnips
6 cloves of garlic, peeled and crushed
juice of ½ lemon
juice and zest of 1 orange
3 tbsp tahini

Charles's advice on growing your own

Borlotti beans

You need a warm summer to succeed with dry beans. When all goes well and you have the harvest by October, they make a fantastic store of dense, protein-rich food for use at any time over the following two years, even. The yield is not high at 0.8kg / m²; however this is extremely dense food which goes a long way.

Grow them as you would any climbing bean. Here we sow them in early May to transplant towards the end of the month. Leave plants unpicked until late September, when you could harvest any pods already brown and dry.

Take a final harvest before early frost and also before the weather is too wet in October. Finish the drying process by spreading them in shallow crates, which you can keep anywhere in the house that is reasonably warm. Once the pods are crisp and dry, you can break them open by first spreading them on a bedsheet on concrete outside, and then walking on them. Many beans fall out; separate the rest from their pods, making sure they are fully dry and hard before storing in jars.

How to rehydrate and cook your beans
After the overnight soak of 5–10 hours, 40 minutes' steady boil for borlotti and 60 minutes for Czar.

Czar white-seeded runner beans

The method for growing is identical to borlotti beans. The main difference is that it's better to harvest the pods of Czar over a period of 3–4 weeks after mid-September, just those that are yellow and reasonably dry. They risk damage from rain once dry, unlike borlotti pods, whose quality when dry is mostly unaffected by rain in late September.

Parsnip

If we did not have potatoes, parsnips would be the go-to winter starchy vegetables. With no dig, they are easy to grow: sow in the surface compost and the taproots go down, even into clay soil. Add a few radish seeds to the drill when you sow, to mark the lines of slower-germinating parsnips.

- Biggest harvests are from sowing around spring equinox. Moist soil means more success for the slowly germinating seeds, and this timing results in a long growing season with yields as high as 7kg / m².
- Also, you can sow right up until early summer, before mid-June. The smaller harvests are balanced by a reduced risk of canker, or rotting of the shoulders. Sowing between garlic in late May is successful.

In wet soils, you can harvest all parsnips in early winter and store them in boxes, crates or paper sacks with the soil still on. Otherwise, leave them in the ground until needed, about late March. Sweetness increases after they have frozen.

Sweet peppers

The overall yield is not high, and in areas with cool summers these are more luxury than staple. They grow well in a 30cm / 12in pot, preferably under cover.

- Sow under cover, from the middle of February and before the end of March. Pepper seedlings need warmth, and the plants require a long season of growth.

You can have unripe, green fruits ready to harvest from July, and by August at a coloured and ripe stage. Autumn can see a relative abundance of peppers, if it stays mild.

Peppers keep for three or four weeks in cool conditions. If picked green but fully developed, they may start to show some colour after a week or two, but with less sweetness than if ripened on the plant.

Ferments
and
vinegars

Classic sauerkraut

Beetroot kvass

Dill pickled cucumbers

Fermented celeriac

Fermented cherry tomatoes

Fermented garlic

Fermented swede and kohlrabi

Elderberry vinegar

Raspberry vinegar

Introduction to ferments and vinegars

In this chapter there are a few ideas of things you can ferment, some of which feature in other recipes in this book. I really encourage you to try and ferment anything that you have a glut of. I was chatting to an allotment neighbour just the other day. I had encouraged him to try fermenting last year and he has really got into it. He recently tried fermenting iceberg lettuce combined with cucumbers, and loves the flavour. I would not have thought of that myself but you just never know until you try. That's the joy of fermentation!

Not only is it a great way to preserve gluts of vegetables, but it is also really beneficial for your health, improving the good bacteria levels in your gut. This brings many benefits, such as improved digestion and better immunity, to name just a couple. Fermenting actually increases the nutritional benefit of your food!

Brine

For some of these recipes I add brine, which is easy to make up yourself. It is important to use filtered water and good quality salt for your brine.

I always use 2% brine, which is 1 litre / 34fl oz of filtered water with 1 tbsp of sea salt, stirred to dilute. You can use lower dilutions if you wish, your finished product will just be more salty to taste. Feel free to experiment to find a taste that you like.

Weights

You will often need to weigh down your vegetables within the jar so they stay submerged under the brine, as anything that comes into contact with oxygen can go mouldy, and that is not what you want. The method I usually use is covering the veg with a firm leaf of some kind, or a slice of the veg, and then putting a smaller jar, also sterilised and filled with water, into the top of the bigger jar. You can also use a clean bag filled with brine, a bag of marbles, or a stone that you have boiled in water for about 15 minutes to sterilise.

Opposite: Fermented swede and kohlrabi

Filderkraut cabbage in October, transplanted in June

Classic sauerkraut

I just can't get enough of this stuff, so tasty and so good for you. It started as a way to use up excess cabbages, and now I make sure I have white cabbages or another light-coloured and tightly packed cabbage growing and available all year round. My favourite cabbages to grow for sauerkraut are Filderkraut (pictured), an old German variety traditionally used for this purpose, although they are tasty any way you use them. They can grow huge. Last year I think my biggest was about 3.5kg / 7lb 11oz (and I know that they can get much bigger than that), so you can make plenty of kraut from just one cabbage.

1. Sterilise a 1 litre / 34fl oz jar and make sure your preparation area, hands, and a large bowl are really clean.

2. Remove the outer leaves from the cabbage (but keep one firm leaf to use as a lid later), then remove the core and shred finely. I recommend using a food processor if you have one: this takes a while by hand and you're less likely to get it as finely cut.

3. Add the cabbage to the bowl with the salt and mix it well, then let it sit for 30–60 minutes until the cabbage is quite wet. Then add the caraway and juniper berries and mix through.

4. Begin to fill your jar by placing a handful of cabbage in the jar and tamping it down firmly. I use the end of a rolling pin for this. Keep adding the cabbage in this way, and when you've used about a third of the cabbage, add one bay leaf, and then another after you've used another third of the cabbage.

5. When all the cabbage has been packed tightly into the jar, there should be about 2–3cm / 1in of space at the top of the jar. You need this space for the water that will be drawn out of your cabbage. Cut your cabbage leaf lid so it will fit tightly into the top of the jar, and then weigh down with your weight of choice (see p.44).

6. Cover it with cloth fixed in place with a tie or rubber band, and leave to ferment from between 1–6 weeks, tasting it occasionally until it has reached the level of ferment that you like. It is important that your cabbage stays completely submerged under the water at all times so keep an eye on it, and top up with 2% brine (see p.44) if needed. Once you've got the flavour you like, take the cloth and the weight off your jar, replace the lid and pop it in the fridge.

Makes 1 x 1 litre / 34fl oz jar

1kg / 2lb 3oz of pale green or white tightly packed cabbage
1 tbsp sea salt
1 tbsp caraway seeds
½ tbsp juniper berries
2 bay leaves

Beetroot kvass

If you have a glut of beetroot then this is definitely worth making. Beetroot kvass is a highly nutritional probiotic drink thought to have originated in the Ukraine, a ferment that exaggerates the health benefits of this fantastic vegetable. It is a tonic for the liver and may help support your immune system, promote gut health and cleanse the blood, among multiple other health benefits. It has a lovely, salty, earthy tanginess with a little fizz to it. Such a lovely drink. I used purple beetroot for the kvass shown in the photo, but you can try it with any colour beetroot you have. The health benefits are much the same but the taste will vary.

1. Chop the beetroot into rough cubes.

2. Place beets into a sterilised 1 litre / 34fl oz jar and add brine, leaving 2cm / 1in at the top of the jar.

3. Cover the jar loosely with muslin or, if using a Kilner-type jar, just remove the rubber seal from the lid and leave for some time to ferment at room temperature. This can be anything from 1–6 weeks, depending on how strong you like your kvass.

4. Keep an eye on it. If scum or mould appears on the top, just remove it with a clean spoon. It may bubble and fizz, but if you have left space at the top of the jar it shouldn't spill over.

5. Taste your kvass every week to see how you like it. The longer you leave it, the stronger the taste will be. I like to leave mine for 6 weeks or so, but I love my ferments pretty strong.

6. Once it has reached the desired flavour / level of fermentation, strain your kvass into a sterilised bottle and keep it in the fridge. It will last a couple of months if you can ration it. I like to have a shot of mine most days. I make it too strong to drink a large glass.

Makes about 1 litre / 34fl oz of kvass

2–3 medium beetroot, washed, skin on
1 litre / 4¼ cups 2% brine (see p.44)

Note
You can reuse the beetroot and fill your jar with brine again to make a second round. When you're done you can eat the beetroot. No need to throw it out, it will still taste lovely even after making you two rounds of kvass. Add it to a salad or just have it on the side. It won't keep very long once it's out of the brine so keep it in the fridge and use it within a couple of days.

Dill pickled cucumbers

No barbeque is complete without this classic ferment. They just taste so good! Luckily they are really easy to make and only take a few days to be ready. I like to use gherkins to make mine, and if you're growing gherkins you are likely to have a pretty good supply throughout the summer. The mistake I make is worrying that I won't have enough, or that one plant will get eaten by slugs when it's a seedling, and then planting too many, resulting in a ridiculously abundant supply of pickles. If you end up in the same position then you will be a very popular guest at many barbeque gatherings.

The key to getting a crisp pickle is soaking them in iced water before, and using the vine or oak leaves to help keep them crisp. These leaves contain a substance that inhibits the enzymes that make pickles soft.

1. Sterilise your jar.

2. Soak your cucumbers or gherkins in iced water for an hour.

3. If you have big gherkins, or you're using cucumbers, then cut them into quarters or long horizontal or vertical slices, making sure they fit standing up in your jar, leaving a 2–3 cm / 1in gap at the top. If you are using baby gherkins then you can leave them whole.

4. Place a vine leaf in the bottom of the jar, with a couple of garlic cloves and some of the dill and mustard seeds. Then tightly pack your cucumbers or gherkins and wedge in your last cloves of garlic and the rest of the dill as you go. Finish with sprinkling in the rest of the mustard seeds: they will fall into the gaps when you add the brine.

5. Then add a vine leaf on top and fill the jar with the brine, and using a spatula, tuck the edges in around the sides of the jar so the leaf is also submerged under the brine. You shouldn't need a weight for these as they should be really tightly packed.

6. Top with a loose-fitting lid. Your ferment needs to breathe so loose fitting is important. If you're using a kilner jar then remove the rubber seal so a little air can get in and out. Leave for 2–3 days then put them in the fridge. They will keep for 2–3 weeks. After that, they will start to go mushy.

Makes 1 x 1 litre / 34fl oz jar of pickles

around 500g / 1lb of gherkins or cucumbers (the weight will vary depending on whether you use small whole gherkins, or sliced cucumber or gherkins); you want to fill a 1 litre / 34 fl oz jar, tightly packed
1 tbsp black mustard seeds
5 cloves of garlic, peeled
small bunch of fresh dill
a couple of young oak leaves or vine leaves
500ml / 2 cups 2% brine (see p.44)

Use what you've grown

As I said above, I grow gherkins specifically so I can make these pickles, but I have also made them with indoor and outdoor cucumbers and they are still totally delicious and moreish. Gherkins are generally a bit more crisp and the plants are usually so abundant you can pick them small and make baby pickles. The bonus with cucumber is one good-sized fruit will fill a jar.

Fermented celeriac

A friend of mine recommended trying this (thank you, Mary) when we were chatting about the joy of fermenting. It is such a lovely flavour and not at all what you would expect. I highly recommend trying this one out, especially if you are sceptical about it. I guarantee you will be pleasantly surprised.

1. Sterilise a 1 litre / 34fl oz jar.

2. Peel and cut the celeriac into small dice, saving a thin, round slice that is about the same size as the inside of your jar. This is to use as a lid later on.

3. Place the celeriac into your jar with the chilli in the middle, leaving a gap of about 2–3cm /1 in at the top. Then pour over your brine and place the slice of celeriac on top, ensuring that it is submerged under the brine. Use a weight (see p.44), and cover with a piece of muslin or thin cloth, then secure with a rubber band or tie.

4. Leave at room temperature for 1–2 weeks, or until it tastes good to you, then keep it in the fridge. It will keep for 6 months or more.

Makes 1 x 1 litre / 34fl oz jar

1kg / 2lb 3oz celeriac
500ml / 2 cups 2% brine
(see p.44)
1 chilli, fresh or dried and
cut in half lengthways

Fermented cherry tomatoes

I just love these. They are quite possibly my favourite ferment. These fizzy, sweet little bursts of scrumptiousness really liven up any kind of salad. If you can manage to save any, it is a great way to get that summery flavour in the colder months when the fresh tomato taste of summer has usually long gone.

1. Sterilise a 1 litre / 34fl oz jar.

2. Prick each tomato with a sharp knife (this will stop the skins from splitting) and stuff them firmly into your jar, adding the basil, garlic and peppercorns intermittently and the bay leaf somewhere in the middle.

3. Pour the 2% brine over your tomatoes and use a weight of your choice (see p.44) to keep the tomatoes under the brine. Cover your jar with a piece of muslin and fix it in place with an elastic band or tie.

4. Leave for 3–5 days at room temperature until they fizz nicely when you pop them in your mouth. Remove your weight and replace the lid, then pop them in the fridge or in a cold store of some sort: they will keep there for months. They may lose their fizz after a couple of months but they will still taste great.

Makes 1 x 1 litre / 34fl oz jar

350g / 12oz cherry tomatoes, or enough to almost fill a 1 litre / 34fl oz jar, leaving a 2–3cm / 1in gap at the top
5 or 6 cloves of garlic
a few sprigs of fresh basil
1 bay leaf
1 tsp black peppercorns
1 litre / 4¼ cups 2% brine (see p.44)

Use what you've grown

You can use bigger tomatoes if that's what you have but you may want to use a 2 litre / 68fl oz jar or bigger as you won't fit many in a smaller jar. When using bigger tomatoes, I also add a few smaller ones to fill the gaps in the jar. If using a bigger jar you will need more brine, enough to cover your tomatoes.

You can try using dill instead of basil, also very tasty. Depending on which herbs you use, the flavour will change slightly. Experiment with different herbs and spices and find a combination that you love.

Note

By refrigerating or putting a ferment in a cold store you only slow down the fermentation process greatly, you can't completely stop it. At home I have an extra fridge which I keep on the coolest setting, and which I use just for storing ferments. At Homeacres, Charles keeps them in a cool room in the house and these kept perfectly well for me to use in salads in spring but were slightly stronger tasting than my fridge-kept ones at home.

Fermented garlic

This recipe is the best way to save garlic if you happen to get white rot. It is just so sad to think that you have to throw all that hard work away, but if you get it out of the ground in good time, and clean it up and ferment it as soon as possible, you will be surprised at how much you can save. You can also ferment healthy garlic – it is not just for bulbs with white rot. It is a great thing to have in the fridge.

The taste is somewhere between roasted and raw garlic and works really well in salad dressings or hummus. You can also use the garlicky brine in the same dishes. There is no point in using it in cooked recipes as cooking any ferment kills the healthy bacteria you have created during the fermentation process.

1. Sterilise your jar.

2. Peel just the loose layers of skin off your garlic. The last layer of skin is the hardest to remove and is perfectly edible after fermentation. If you are using part-rotted garlic, then be sure to remove any skin or part of the clove that has rot on it. You can cut bits off cloves if needed. Save whatever you can.

3. Place the cloves into your sterilised jar and cover with the brine. Add a weight (see p.44), cover with muslin and secure with an elastic band or tie, then leave to ferment for 4–6 weeks. Once they are fermented, store in the fridge. They will keep for a year or more. Don't worry if some cloves turn a little blue – this sometimes happens during the fermentation process and is perfectly normal.

Makes a 500ml / 17fl oz jar

as much garlic as you want / need to ferment; 6 full bulbs will make roughly enough to fill a 500ml / 17fl oz jar

enough 2% brine (see p.44) to cover your garlic; if you are using a 500ml / 17fl oz jar, then make up 500ml / 17fl oz brine

Fermented swede and kohlrabi

For this recipe I am using half and half swede and kohlrabi, but if you have a bit more of one than the other it doesn't really matter. Just remember the different flavours you are combining, the sweetness of the swede and the gentle pepperiness of the kohlrabi, if you alter the ratio then you will change the flavour of your finished ferment.

1. Before you prep your veg for fermentation, think about what you will use as a lid to stop any veg floating to the top and being exposed to oxygen. Fermentation happens when the veg is completely covered. Anything exposed to oxygen will rot and you don't want that. I use a thin slice or two from the middle of whichever vegetable is best suited in shape. If you grate your veg before you remember (like I often do), you can always use a firm cabbage leaf instead (see photo opposite, where I used a red cabbage leaf as a lid, giving the top layer a pinky tinge). This will not affect the flavour.

2. Sterilise a 1 litre / 34fl oz jar.

3. Grate the swede and kohlrabi and combine in a bowl with the salt and the dill seed, mix well and leave for half an hour. This allows time for the salt to start to draw the water out of the vegetables.

4. Take your sterilised jar and place a bit of the grated veg in the bottom, then stamp it down firmly with the end of a rolling pin or something similar and repeat this until you've used up all the veg. You should have 2–3cm / 1in of space still at the top of the jar. The salt should have drawn out some water from the veg.

5. Place your vegetable lid on top of the grated veg and weigh it down (see p.44), then cover with a small piece of muslin cloth and fix with an elastic band. If the liquid is not covering the veg within 30 minutes to 1 hour, then add some brine (see p.44).

6. Leave to stand for at least a week and taste it. If you like it as it is, then pop it in the fridge and enjoy. If you would like it a bit stronger, then leave for another week and taste it again. I leave mine for about 6 weeks as I like my ferments really strong, but it is all about personal taste.

Makes 1 x 1 litre / 34fl oz jar

350g / 12oz swede
350g / 12oz kohlrabi, purple or green is fine
1 tbsp sea salt
1 tbsp dill seed

Elderberry vinegar

There is nothing I like more than something that tastes great and is like medicine for my body. Homegrown food generally falls into this category, depending on how you prepare it, but some things, like this vinegar, I actively use as medicine. Elderberries are rich in antioxidants and vitamins, and they have traditionally been used as a preventative and treatment for colds and flu. Nature gives these amazing berries to us in the autumn, just in time to be consumed regularly through the winter months when our bodies need that vitamin boost to keep us healthy. I also make elderberry cordial with cloves and a mug of this, warm with a dash of vinegar, is a delicious and comforting winter drink. You can also have the vinegar on its own in hot water daily, to boost your immunity.

Like other fruit vinegars, it also goes well drizzled over ice cream for a little treat, or used in a salad dressing. This vinegar can also be used in hot dishes, adding a depth of flavour to a tomato-based sauce or a stir fry.

1. Place berries in a large bowl or jar, mash them slightly and cover with the vinegar. Leave to stand for about 5 days.

2. Strain the elderberries through a sieve lined with muslin, gather up the edges and squeeze out as much juice / vinegar as you can. Place the vinegar in a saucepan with the sweetener, then bring to the boil and simmer for 10 minutes.

Makes about 1 litre / 4 ¼ cups

450g / 1lb de-stemmed elderberries
600ml / 2 ½ cups cider vinegar
300g / 11oz xylitol (birch sugar) or sugar

Safety note

Make sure that the elderberries you use are fully ripe. You can use a fork to remove them from their stems. The stems and green berries are poisonous so remove as many of these as possible. A few of the tiny stems will inevitably be left. Don't worry too much about this as you will be straining them out anyway.

You should never consume raw elderberries as they are poisonous. Boiling the berries makes them perfectly safe for consumption.

Raspberry vinegar

The first time I made this vinegar, I was apprehensive about using so many of my precious raspberries as I love eating them so much and always feel that I never have enough. However, I had absolutely no regrets. Just a little of this in a salad dressing, or even drizzled over ice cream (sounds odd but it really works), brings that fresh raspberry flavour into lots of dishes. I always use xylitol in my flavoured vinegars as I like to keep my sugar intake down, and as it's vinegar, you don't need the preserving qualities that sugar brings. You can use sugar instead if that suits you better.

1. Place the raspberries in a large bowl or jug. In a saucepan, combine the vinegar and sweetener and heat gently until the sweetener is dissolved. Make sure you do not boil your vinegar.

2. Pour the warm vinegar over the raspberries and mash them slightly. Cover and leave to sit for 2 days to a week.

3. Line a sieve with muslin and strain the vinegar into a bowl, then gather up the edges of the muslin and give it a good squeeze to get as much tasty juice as you can out of the raspberries. If you particularly want a clear vinegar, then don't squeeze the raspberries in the cloth as this will make the vinegar cloudy and, once settled, will leave a residue at the bottom of your bottle. I personally like to get as much liquid as I can out of my raspberries, so I squeeze it until I can squeeze no more.

4. Transfer your vinegar into a clean bottle and store in a cool, dry place.

Makes about 850ml / 3 ½ cups

450g / 1lb fresh or frozen raspberries
600ml / 2 ½ cups cider vinegar
115g / 4oz xylitol (birch sugar) or sugar

Use what you've grown

A couple of years ago I was a little short on raspberries, so I used half and half raspberries and redcurrants and it worked really well. You can try making flavoured vinegars out of any berries or currants. You may want to increase the amount of sugar for a more tart berry, but try it and see. If you're scared of trying something and wasting produce then make a small amount first and see what happens.

Charles's advice on growing your own

Beetroot

Homegrown beetroot tick all the boxes. They are sweet and flavoursome, easy and quick to grow in both cool and warmer climates, and have a long season of growth and storage. It's possible to eat this wonderful food for 10–11 months of the year.

In addition, you can harvest 8kg / m^2 or even more. Large beets in no dig soil are tender and juicy: any woodiness of texture would be from using synthetic fertilisers.

- Multisow firstly in late winter if not too cold, otherwise early spring is fine. Here I find that 1st March is reliable, always under cover.
- The last sowing date depends on your level of autumn warmth; here it's late June, for large roots to store. Later sowings still work, if you are happy with small beetroot. I would try a few dates to see what's good for you.

Growth is rapid in summer, when seed to harvest can be as little as 60 days.

Pick at any size according to your preference.

Beetroot stores for up to five months through winter. Leave some soil on the roots and keep in a cool shed.

Cabbage

Homegrown cabbage, when no synthetic fertiliser is used, is tender and full of fine flavour. Plus there are cabbages for all seasons! They are easy in cool and warmer climates, with a long season of growth. In a temperate climate, it's possible to cut a cabbage almost any month of the year.

Sowing time varies, according to the variety you are growing. These dates are a broad outline and you can use them to discover the absolute best dates for your climate.

- Seeds sown in late winter to early spring will harvest in late spring to early summer.
- Seeds sown in late spring will harvest in autumn.
- Seeds sown in midsummer will harvest in winter to early spring.
- Seeds sown in late summer will harvest in mid- to late spring.

Beetroot Boltardy in August, from a June multisowing

Firm heads of cabbage store impressively well when the temperature is below 10°C / 50°F, and cooler is good. Winter cabbage heads will stand frosts of about -5°C / 23°F, while green cabbages stand much colder than that. You can store cabbage as sauerkraut (see p.47).

Yields can be good, from 3kg / m² in early summer, to twice that for autumn cabbage hearts. Pick at any size or stage, according to your preference. Hearts have sweeter leaves.

Celeriac

There's a lot of flavour in a small amount of homegrown celeriac. Keep a large one in the kitchen, because even after cutting bits off they are good to use for over two weeks.

The dense roots are full of goodness and store well through winter, even into the hungry gap. They taste great in salads and pickles, grated or chopped small.

You may harvest as much as 4kg / m², but this is not the easiest vegetable to succeed with in growing. Don't overwater them in summer, give more in autumn.

Mid- to late March in warmth is best for sowing, because celeriac needs the whole season to grow large. Buying plants in May is an option if you miss the March sowing, or don't have a protected space for propagation.

Harvests happen through autumn. I recommend you harvest by Christmas, for less damage caused by disease, rodents and slugs.

When storing celeriac, don't trim the base too tight. Leaving some moist compost and soil between the many small roots helps to keep them plump. Simply store in a box. You can eat celeriac any time until early spring, after trimming.

Kohlrabi

These are beautiful plants, floating their swelling stems above the ground. When harvested young and tender, they can be sweet as well as very tasty. Their texture also is firm, more so than the closely related turnip.

There are two periods of growth, separated by their flowering time of summer.
- Sowings in late February can provide about six weeks of harvest before midsummer.
- Summer sowings can give up to six months of harvest, plus the possibility of storage in autumn and winter.

Yields vary hugely according to how large you let them grow, and the time of year. Harvests of late autumn store well, but become woody at base level when kept a long time. Just pare this off before preparing them.

Azur Star kohlrabi, early June

Swede

Swedes are the bass notes of winter. They are biennial, so they overwinter as a root and then flower in the spring. They are descended from turnips, and share some characteristics.

Two differences from turnips are:

- Swedes have just the one sowing time – end of May to early June, for winter harvests.
- The texture of swedes is denser and sweeter.

Many insects can devour and spoil swedes when they are small. Therefore sow in modules under cover, plant out after four weeks, and keep them covered with mesh for at least the first four weeks outside.

That's the hard part done, then they almost look after themselves. Remove a few outer leaves every week, to reduce slug numbers.

They store well in the ground because of their hardiness. Or you can harvest in December and keep them anywhere cool and damp. There may be some cabbage root fly maggots eating the outsides, and you just trim off that damage.

The first root vegetables of early summer

Salads

Borlotti bean and tomato salad

Cabbage and carrot slaw

Carrot, beetroot and apple salad

Celeriac remoulade

Courgette, carrot and pea salad
with peanut dressing

Cucumber, celery and elderflower salad

Heirloom tomatoes with basil and garlic

Kale and raspberry salad

Rocket, carrot and spiced chickpea salad

Kohlrabi slaw

Tabbouleh

Borlotti bean and tomato salad

This is a great way to bring a zesty summery taste to the winter months and a great one for the hungry gap, using all the things that you've preserved in various ways from your summer harvests. Of course, it is not strictly a winter salad. You can replace the fermented and dried tomatoes with fresh ones, and have a lovely bean salad in the summer instead. That is, if you still have any beans left. I've usually used all mine by this point, or put them back in the ground as the next season's seed.

1. In a small bowl, mix the cumin, lemon juice and olive oil.
2. Add the dressing to your cooked borlotti beans, along with the rest of the ingredients, and mix well. If you have a bit of juice on the chopping board from your fermented tomatoes then add that too. They're all going to be nice flavours for your beany salad.

Serves 4–6 as a side dish

¾ tsp ground cumin
juice of ½ lemon
2 tbsp extra virgin olive oil
500g / 1 lb cooked borlotti
    beans (see p.40), or about
    2 tins drained beans
175g / 6oz fermented tomatoes,
    chopped (see p.52)
20g / 0.75oz dried tomatoes,
    chopped, no need to soak
4 spring or red onions, chopped
2 tbsp chopped, fresh coriander

Use what you've grown

I do lots of variations on this salad for Homeacres course lunches. The basic ingredients are cooked beans (borlotti or Czar), any ferment that you want to use (I like krauted cabbage or beetroot), red or spring onions, and fresh parsley or another herb that will work alongside your choice of ferment, with a little oil for dressing to finish it off. The cumin and lemon juice I use here are only for the tomato version.

Cabbage and carrot slaw

This is a classic combination, and for good reason. I am not really a fan of mayonnaise on coleslaw so this is my take on an old favourite.

1. Finely slice your cabbage and onion, grate your carrot, and then mix together in a large bowl.

2. Add the cider vinegar to your veg, mix well, and leave to stand for 30 minutes.

3. Combine the mustard, oil, garlic and honey together and mix well.

4. Add the dressing to the veg with the parsley, and stir to combine.

Serves 6–8 as a side dish

2 tbsp cider vinegar
2 tbsp wholegrain mustard
4 tbsp olive oil
1 clove of garlic
1 tsp honey
450g / 1lb white cabbage, quartered, cores removed
300g / 11oz carrots
1 small red onion, halved
2 tbsp chopped parsley
salt and pepper to taste

Use what you've grown

Really you can use any light-coloured cabbage. White cabbage is classic but not essential. I have used the hearts of spring cabbages, which works well, or red cabbage is a great alternative. You could also replace some or all of the carrot with beetroot of any colour, and if it's early in the season you can use 3–4 spring onions instead of the red onion. White onion will also work fine, but is a little stronger in flavour so you may want to use a bit less.

Carrot, beetroot and apple salad

Super simple and super tasty, this is a Homeacres favourite. I always make plenty of it and the bowl is always empty at the end of lunch. The ingredients ratio will differ greatly depending on what is available (see 'Use what you've grown' below).

I am a firm believer in not peeling anything unless it is absolutely necessary. There are so many nutrients in the skin itself, and just below the surface of the skin, and if you have grown it yourself (especially if you have used the no dig method), then you know there are no nasties in the soil. Plus there is the added benefit of saving time, so you can be outside in your garden!

1. Wash and grate the beetroot, carrot and apple.

2. Finely chop the mint.

3. Add everything to a large bowl with the lemon juice, and give it a good stir to mix.

Serves 4 as a side dish

250g / 9oz beetroot
150g / 5oz carrots
100g / 3.5oz apples,
    cores removed
small bunch of fresh mint
juice of 1 lemon

Use what you've grown

This is a very versatile salad. You can add more or less carrot or beetroot depending on what you have and what you want to use up. I would quite happily use a similar ratio of beetroot to carrot, or more carrot than beetroot, although you do really want the beetroot to have a leading role in this salad. I only add apples when they are available. If you store them right, then this can be for 6 months of the year or more. If you don't have apples, this salad works just fine with only carrots and beetroot.

Courgette, carrot and pea salad with peanut dressing

Celeriac remoulade

What I love most about this dish is that so many people tell me they don't like celeriac, but they like this dish. It is such a quick and easy salad to make and a hit with just about everyone.

I always use freshly made aioli to make my remoulade, but if you don't want to be eating raw eggs or are short on time, you can replace it with mayonnaise. But be warned, it will not be as delicious (although still very tasty).

1. Place the the aioli, lemon juice and mustard in a small bowl, and whisk together until smooth.
2. Add the dressing to your grated celeriac with the parsley, if using, and mix well. Add salt and pepper to taste.

Serves 4 as a side dish

1 celeriac, about 450g / 1lb, peeled and grated
6 tbsp aioli (see p.21)
1 tbsp Dijon mustard
2 tbsp lemon juice
1 tbsp chopped parsley, if available
salt and pepper to taste

Courgette, carrot and pea salad with peanut dressing

This is a lovely, fresh spring salad. The first of the courgettes and peas with this Oriental-style dressing is a great way to welcome in the first harvests of the new growing season. It goes really well as a side dish with a stir fry or Thai curry.

1. First, make your dressing: combine the peanut butter, tamari, oils, lime juice and water in a small jug or bowl, and mix until you have a smooth dressing.
2. Wash and grate the courgettes and carrots. Top and tail the sugar snap peas and cut them in half, then combine them in a bowl with the grated veg.
3. Add the dressing to the veg and stir well to combine, then top with the toasted sesame seeds.

Serves 6 as a side dish

3 tbsp peanut butter
1 tbsp tamari
1 tbsp toasted sesame oil
1 tbsp sesame oil
juice of one lime
2 tbsp water
400g / 14oz courgettes
400g / 14oz carrots
200g / 7oz sugar snap peas
2 tbsp toasted sesame seeds

Use what you've grown

Instead of sugar snap peas you can use mangetout or even lightly cooked fresh peas. This salad can also work well with only the carrot and courgette. If you have fresh red chillis and you like a little spice, you can always slice one thinly and add it to the dressing.

Cucumber, celery and elderflower salad

This is such a delightful summer salad. The elderflower cordial dressing works so perfectly with the cucumber and celery.

I always make my own cordial and I make sure I have enough to keep some in the fridge to use for dressings and other treats. If you don't have room in the fridge, then you can put it in ice cube trays and pop it in the freezer to defrost as and when you need it. If you don't make it, or if you missed the season for elderflowers, then off-the-shelf elderflower cordial will work just fine.

1. Firstly, make your dressing. Combine the cordial, oil, vinegar, mustard and honey in a jar, and give it a good shake to mix.

2. Finely slice the cucumber and the celery. I recommend using a mandoline or a blender with a fine slicing attachment so you get the slices really thin. If you want to, you can peel your cucumber, as the skin is too bitter for some. As I have mentioned before, I would rather eat the nutrients that are in the skin than put them back in the compost heap, but make it as you like it.

3. Finely chop the herbs, place in a large bowl, and mix in with the cucumber and celery.

4. Add the dressing to the bowl and mix well. Leave to rest in the fridge for about an hour, mixing occasionally.

Serves 6–8 as a side dish

3 tbsp elderflower cordial
3 tbsp olive oil
2 tsp cider vinegar
1 tsp Dijon mustard
1 tsp honey
1 cucumber
4 sticks celery
small bunch of parsley
small bunch of mint
a few fronds of dill

Use what you've grown

The basic recipe needs to stay the same here, but you can vary the herbs a little, depending on what you have. I recommend always having mint in there, but you can put more, less or none of the dill and parsley. If you are feeling adventurous, you could try something entirely different. This will obviously change the flavour, but you never know what will work until you try it.

Red and yellow Brandywine and Berner Rose tomatoes, with basil and garlic

Heirloom tomatoes with basil and garlic

This is so simple but it looks amazing on the table. If you are growing your own tomatoes, then it is a great way to show them off. If you've got different colours then even better, but it's not essential – they will still taste great. Using good quality oil and salt makes a lot of difference in this recipe so don't cut corners here. Do your glorious homegrown tomatoes justice and splash out on the good stuff. You won't regret it.

1. Make your dressing first: combine the oil, garlic, basil and salt. Mix well and leave to stand for at least 30 minutes to let the flavours infuse.

2. Remove the stem root from the top of the tomatoes. These are tough and stringy so best to get rid of them. Then slice the tomatoes horizontally so they hold together.

3. Arrange the tomatoes on a plate, fanning them round in a nice pattern. If you have different-coloured fruit, then you can get creative to make it look really stunning.

4. Drizzle the dressing over the tomatoes so there is a little on every slice. Try not to drown them. You can always save the basil and garlic oil in the fridge and use it another day. It will keep well for a few days.

Serves 4–6 as a side dish

2 tbsp extra virgin olive oil
4 cloves of garlic, crushed
bunch of basil leaves, chopped
½ tsp good quality salt
2–3 beef or extra large variety tomatoes (depending on the size), different colours if you have them

Use what you've grown

If you don't have large beefy-type tomatoes, then you can use a combination of tomatoes of other sizes. If I am using smaller tomatoes, I still remove the stem root, but you don't need to do this if using cherry tomatoes. If you want to make a bruschetta-style dish, chop them into large chunks and put into a bowl with the garlic, basil and oil, then mix well. Serve on some toasted sourdough or crusty bread making sure you drizzle the juice over the top so the tomato juice soaks into the bread... yummmmm!

Kale and raspberry salad

This is just a glorious summer salad. You might think that you have to cook kale, but after making this salad you will know the joy of eating it raw. Put it with some fresh raspberries, feta cheese and a light and fruity dressing, and I assure you this will become a favourite for the duration of your raspberry season.

1. Make the dressing first by adding the vinegar, mustard, honey, and 1 tbsp olive oil to a jar, screw on the lid tightly and give it a good shake until it's all well combined.

2. Cut the large veins out of the kale leaves and roughly chop into bite-sized pieces.

3. Place in a large bowl with the remaining olive oil and the salt, and massage the oil and salt into the leaves thoroughly, making every effort to get oil into all the nooks and crannies of your kale leaves. This will take a few minutes. The more you massage the kale, the more tender it will be.

4. Crumble in the feta cheese, and take half the raspberries then crush them a little before adding to the kale and cheese. Add the rest of the raspberries and the dressing, and gently toss to coat.

5. Sprinkle with the toasted sunflower seeds before serving.

Serves 4 as a side dish

2 tbsp raspberry vinegar
  (see p.57)
1 tsp Dijon mustard
1 tsp honey
3 tbsp olive oil
350g / 12oz kale
1 tsp good quality salt
150g / 5oz fresh raspberries
120g / 4oz feta cheese
4 tbsp sunflower seeds, toasted

Use what you've grown

I like to use curly kale if I have it, but you can use any kale you have. It will be slightly different in texture and flavour but still really good. I have tried it with cavolo nero and red kale, and both worked perfectly.

Rocket, carrot and spiced chickpea salad

Rocket, carrot and spiced chickpea salad

You might be thinking 'yet another salad with carrots!', but they are so good and versatile, and just so nice and crunchy when raw. The orange juice in this dressing is a lovely compliment to the carrots, with that little touch of honey to bring out the sweetness.

1. First, make your dressing: combine tahini, yogurt and orange juice in a small jug or bowl, and whisk until smooth.

2. Heat the oil over a medium heat, then add the spices, garlic, sultanas and chickpeas and cook for 3–4 minutes until the chickpeas are warm. Turn the heat off and add the honey to the pan, stirring until it is well mixed in.

3. Wash and grate the carrots, then add to a large bowl with the chickpeas and dressing, and mix until well combined. Then add your rocket and coriander, if using, and stir gently before serving.

Serves 4 as a side dish

1 tbsp olive oil
1 tsp ground cumin
½ tsp ground coriander
2–4 cloves of garlic, depending on how much you like garlic
250g / 9oz cooked chickpeas (this is about one drained can)
60g / 2oz sultanas
1 tbsp honey
3 carrots
1½ tbsp tahini
75ml / ⅓ cup yogurt (I use my homemade, kefir yogurt but any plain yogurt will do fine)
3 tbsp orange juice
85g / 3oz wild rocket leaves
1 tbsp fresh coriander (if you have it)

Kohlrabi slaw

I love growing these funny-looking members of the cabbage family, and this slaw is a great way to use them. If the leaves are good, then put a few of them in too.

1. Start by making your dressing: combine the aioli, oil, vinegar, mustard and celery seeds in a small bowl or jug, and mix until smooth.

2. Grate the kohlrabi and finely slice the cabbage, celery and spring onion.

3. Combine the veg with the dressing and mix well.

Serves 4 as a side dish

2–3 heaped dessert spoonfuls of aioli (see p.21) or mayonnaise
2 tbsp olive oil
2 tbsp cider vinegar
1 tbsp wholegrain mustard
Continued on next page

Use what you've grown

A slaw is super versatile, so make it work with what you've got. The basics are the kohlrabi and cabbage, but other than that you can be inventive. I would quite happily add a mooli or other mild radish instead of the celery. The spring onions are optional, but if you like an onion in your slaw then red onion or a shallot would also work well. Just make sure only to add a little, so as not to overpower the other veg.

½ tsp celery seeds
450g / 1lb kohlrabi, red or green
200g / 7oz cabbage, white or red, quartered and cores removed
1 stick celery
1 spring onion, optional
salt and pepper to taste

Tabbouleh

I love tabbouleh. It is a fresh, zingy salad packed full of parsley, which works well on any salad spread. It is originally a Middle Eastern dish, traditionally containing bulgar wheat, lots of herbs and tomato, but in my version, I prefer to use quinoa and more vegetables than would be typical. After all that's what it's all about in this book. It also works well using couscous or freekeh as your grain, but use whatever you prefer or have in the cupboard. You just need something that will soak up the dressing and juices.

1. Make the dressing by combining the oil, lemon juice then garlic in a jar, giving it a shake to combine.

2. To cook your quinoa, start by rinsing it in a mesh sieve for a couple of minutes while agitating it with your fingers. This removes the natural outer layer, which can create a slightly bitter taste. Add 180ml / ¾ cup of water and bring it to the boil, then cover with a lid and simmer for 15–20 minutes, or until the water has been absorbed. Leave to cool.

3. Remove the stems from the mint and parsley and finely chop.

4. Finely dice the cucumber, tomato and onion.

5. In a large bowl, combine all of the ingredients and mix well. If the quinoa (or whatever grain you have used) is still a little warm, then it will really absorb the dressing, not straight from the stove and hot, though, as you want your herbs and veggies to be fresh and crunchy. Refrigerate for at least a couple of hours, or even overnight before serving. This will give some time to let the flavours really infuse.

Serves 4–6 as a side dish

4 tbsp olive oil
3–4 tbsp lemon juice
2 cloves of garlic, crushed
60g / 2oz quinoa or grain of your choice
200g / 7oz cucumber
200g / 7oz tomato
½ small red onion
40g / 1.4oz fresh parsley, flat leaf or curly is fine
40g / 1.4oz fresh mint

Use what you've grown

You can play with the tomato and cucumber ratio depending on what you have. You could use fresh gherkins or cucamelons as a cucumber alternative, but there is no replacement for tomatoes. Saying that, you can always just leave them out if you don't have any. You could also replace the red onion with spring onions.

Charles's advice on growing your own

Spring onions

This vegetable excites me in the spring, for its new green shoots which are so lush and health-giving. I value the green more than the white, although both are wonderful in so many dishes. Onion leaves and raw garlic take breakfast muesli to a new level!

One sowing gives harvests over a long period. Multisow up to ten seeds for clumps averaging eight onions, planted at 20–25cm / 8–10in. The close spacing, coupled with all growth being edible, makes for a lot to eat, even 5kg / m² when harvested at a medium or even large size.

- Sow under cover in late winter, and secondly in late spring.

This interval of a whole three months should assure continuity of picking lovely green onions. Later harvests from any sowing will be larger and with some bulb, still good for eating raw but with green leaves less tender.

- You can sow salad onions in summer, but their autumn maturity carries a risk of mildew on the leaves.
- Best of all, multisow White Lisbon in late August. Transplant these where space becomes available through September, to overwinter as small plants. They are hardy and don't need protection.

French and runner beans, dwarf and climbing

Flavour is a big motivation for growing your own, plus the regularity of harvests over a long period. Pick small or large, according to how you like them.

You can grow prolific harvests in summer, but these plants do not thrive in cool conditions. Their overriding need is for warmth, therefore wait to sow under cover until the middle of May, and outside in early June. You can sow until early July.

They are all sensitive to frost, so the harvest period for fresh pods is midsummer to early autumn, around three months. For dry pods, it's early to mid-autumn and before the first frost.

The flowers are salad rocket, edible and spicy

They are space efficient for two reasons. The yield is from 2kg / m² for dwarf beans to 6kg / m² for climbing beans. And dwarf beans are quick to crop, in as little as 50 days from sowing in summer, so they are good to plant after spring harvests finish of beetroot, carrots, spinach etc.

Celery

Chopped, homegrown celery stalks add wonderful flavour and texture, to salads in particular. Bought celery has usually been grown with synthetic fertilisers and maximum amounts of water to increase growth. The look is impressive and its texture is tender, but the flavour is reduced.

An early sowing will stand right through until autumn, but its stems become more fibrous and new growth happens as sideshoots. A sowing in late spring is therefore worthwhile.

- Celery sown in early spring will give harvests of heads through summer.
- Celery sown in mid- to late spring will give harvests of heads through autumn.
- In warm climates, a third celery sowing is possible during summer, for harvests into winter, as long as frosts are only slight.

Celery heads can be stood upright in a large cup or glass, with 2.5 cm / 1in of water. They draw on the water to keep their stems crisp. Cut off some celery to use as needed, for up to a week after harvest.

Plants are space efficient, with a yield of up to 5kg / m².

Cucumber

Feedback from my customers in the local town of Bruton suggests there is little flavour in supermarket cucumbers. They say 'Your cucumbers taste like they used to!' Certainly they are sweeter and juicier from being fresh, and grown in soil rather than hydroponically. The season of harvests is July to September.

They are easy to grow if your climate is warm. Avoid sowing too early: my first sowing date is the middle of April, strictly in the greenhouse.

- Cordon varieties, sown under cover in mid-spring and grown under cover, are ready to harvest in early summer to late autumn.
- Ridge varieties, sown under cover in mid- to late spring, and grown outside, are ready to harvest in midsummer to very early autumn. They have knobbly skin which you may want to slice off, and growth is prolific in warm weather, giving up to 5kg / m² over just two months.

Nature has given cucumbers a lovely wrapper of skin. They can store for up to a week at temperatures below 15°C / 59°F. A limp cucumber is still good to eat, just less moist.

Tomatoes in the polytunnel, mid–August

Tomatoes

Tomatoes can be grown in many ways, and you can fit them into almost any growing situation. Read about and choose from a wonderful range of varieties, to find your preferred plant and fruit size, colour and the flavours you like. They will compare favourably to most you can buy.

There are two main types, so check you know which are which when growing.

- Cordon or indeterminate plants, for growing vertically and with support in a protected or sheltered area.
- Bush or determinate plants for growing on the ground or in containers.

Cherry tomatoes are great for sweet snacks. Larger and beef tomatoes give more weight of harvest, up to 8kg / m² in warm conditions.

The rapidly increasing light and warmth of spring make later sowings far easier to manage. I sow in mid-March, for planting under cover in May. For outdoor growing, I sow and plant two weeks later. Sungold F1 is my earliest harvest in June, if it's been warm, while beef tomatoes crop from about mid-July under cover.

You can harvest large tomatoes at the first sign of notable colour, called 'breaking stage'. This does not reduce flavour, and allows plants to put more energy into new fruits. Cherry tomatoes are best when ripened on the plant.

In your house, tomatoes keep better on the counter than in the fridge. Fully grown tomatoes picked green in October, when you need to clear the plants, will store for at least a month in ambient house warmth, while slowly ripening.

Cherry tomatoes can be frozen whole in polythene bags. Tomatoes are excellent for canning / sterilising in glass jars, in a water bath at near-boiling temperature.

Storing and drying tomatoes

By Charles

My preferred way to store tomatoes is by dehydration. Some people call this 'sun-dried', but often that description is applied to electric dehydration. It's difficult to get enough energy from sunlight in late summer and early autumn, to remove the 95% of water from slices of tomato. That is the weight difference I measure from beef and large tomatoes, before and after drying. The precise weight loss varies with weather and season.

This method enables you to preserve a very small volume of intense flavour. It just needs a decent amount of energy to extract that 95% of water. I use a 9-rack box with heater and fan, set at 52°C / 125°F for up to 12 hours.

Slice the tomatoes as thinly as you can, which is about 6mm / 0.25in with a sharp knife. Pack them in really tightly together on the racks, because they shrink very quickly as they lose volume.

After at least eight hours, check for moisture content by lifting a slice and bending it. It should be tight and stiff, rather than soft and jelly-like.

These slices are dense and chewy. You can pack a lot in jars to store for as long as you wish.

By Catherine

I part-dry my tomatoes in the oven and store them in olive oil, as I don't have room for a dehydrator in my tiny kitchen.

To semi-dry your tomatoes, preheat the oven to 120°C / 250°F fan, cut them in half and place them cut side up on a baking tray lined with greaseproof paper, tightly packing them onto the tray. If you have beef tomatoes, cut them into fat slices. Brush them with a little olive oil, season with salt and pepper and sprinkle with a little dried oregano, trying to get a tiny bit on each tomato half. Place them in the oven and don't close the oven properly, but leave it very slightly ajar. This is so any moisture can escape. Cook them for about 3–4 hours until semi-dried.

Once cool, pack them tightly into jars and fill the jars with olive oil, making sure you fully cover the tomatoes. If fully covered, they will keep in a cool, dry place for 6 months. Once opened, store in the fridge and use within a couple of weeks. Once you've used your tomatoes, you can use the leftover oil in salad dressings.

Cooked salads

Beetroot, fennel and potato salad

Aubergine rolls

Algarvian carrots

Beetroot, squash and feta salad

Broad bean, pea and feta salad

Chard and white bean salad

Beetroot, fennel and potato salad

This dish goes on the menu as soon as the fennel bulbs are ready in late spring, and if you have a summer planting of fennel, then it can be had again in the autumn. It always goes down a storm at the course lunches, and it's a great alternative way to have potatoes, perfect as a hot or cold salad. An all-round winner!

1. Preheat the oven to 200°C / 390°F fan. Wash the beetroot and potatoes (no need to peel), chop your potatoes in half or quarters, depending on the size, and the beetroot slightly bigger, again depending on the size. Place in a large bowl and add 3 tbsp oil, seasoning and the fresh thyme. Stir to coat.

2. Place on a baking tray and roast for about half an hour, or until the potatoes are nicely cooked and just starting to brown around the edges. Beetroot cooking time is not so important, as they can be eaten raw and are nice when they still have a bit of crunch.

3. Meanwhile, trim and chop the fennel into chunks. Heat 2 tbsp oil in a frying pan, and fry until nicely cooked and starting to brown at the edges.

4. Combine 3 tbsp oil, lemon zest and juice, and the honey with a little salt and pepper in a jar, seal with a lid, and give a good shake until well mixed.

5. Place the cooked ingredients, the dressing and the rocket into a large bowl and stir gently to combine. If you are serving this cold, then wait until just before serving to do this step so your rocket leaves are nice and fresh. They will wilt alongside the hot food, which works when it's all hot, but you want your rocket to still have that raw crunch when serving it cold.

Serves 6–8 as a side dish

400g / 14oz new potatoes
600g / 1lb 5oz beetroot
8 tbsp olive oil
a few sprigs of fresh thyme
2 good-sized fennel bulbs
 bunch of wild rocket
zest and juice of 1 lemon
1 tsp honey
salt and pepper to taste

Use what you've grown

The taste of early beetroots and new potatoes is much fresher and lighter. However, this dish is still really tasty when made with older potatoes and beetroot. You can also use normal rocket rather than wild rocket. It won't be as peppery but still good. Alternatively, you can use any peppery salad leaf if that's what you have, like mustard greens.

Aubergine rolls

These are so easy and look so nice on the table served on a bed of lettuce or rocket: something I like to bring to any 'bring a dish' meal while aubergines are in season. It looks like you've made a big effort, but if you've already got pesto in the fridge they are super quick to make. You want long and fat aubergines for this to work best.

If you want to make it vegan, then replace the cheese with oven-roasted or sun-blushed tomato, one per roll.

1. Slice your aubergines lengthways into roughly 1cm / 0.5in slices. Place them on the grill pan, brush with oil, and season with salt and pepper on both sides. Grill for 3–5 minutes until lightly brown. Turn the slices over, and brown on the other side. Leave to cool.

2. Spread each aubergine slice with a thin coating of pesto (about 1 tsp per slice) and a small dollop of cheese, then roll, starting from the smaller end.

3. If you need to, you can pin with a cocktail stick so they stay together until serving.

Serves 6 as starter or side dish

olive oil for drizzling
2–3 large aubergines, depending on size
120g / 4oz ready-made pesto of your choice (see p.24)
150g / 3oz soft cheese of your choice; I use homemade kefir cheese, but cream cheese or cottage cheese works well too

Algarvian carrots

I picked up this recipe while on holiday in a sweet little fishing village in Portugal. It was so tasty, and great to have a cooked carrot salad for a change. It's also great as a tapas option if you're a veggie. I recommend making this ahead of time and keeping it in the fridge for a few days to a week, so the flavours really soak into the carrots. A good recipe for a more mature crop of carrots.

1. Bring a pot of water to the boil. Scrub the carrots and put them whole into the boiling water. Cook them for 8–10 minutes so they are soft on the outside and still a little crunchy in the middle.

2. While they are cooking, make the marinade. De-stem and finely chop the parsley and coriander. Crush the garlic and add this and the herbs to a large bowl with the oil, vinegar and cumin, and stir well to combine.

3. When the carrots are done, drain them. While they are still hot, chop them into bite-sized pieces, then add to the bowl with the marinade and stir well, so the carrots are fully coated. Adding the carrots to the marinade when warm will mean they absorb much more of it.

4. Place in a sterilised jar and keep in the fridge. Bring them out of the fridge one hour before you serve.

Serves 6 as a side dish

6–8 large carrots
2–6 cloves of garlic, depending on taste
small bunch of fresh coriander
small bunch of fresh parsley
2 tsp cumin
115ml / ½ cup olive oil
3 tbsp red / white wine or cider vinegar

Beetroot, squash and feta salad

This is so easy and always goes down so well on the no dig course lunches, with people often naming it as their favourite dish. It just goes to show that tasty food does not have to be complicated, need lots of ingredients or take a long time. I make plenty of this as it is so popular but it is very easy to scale down or up, depending on how many you are feeding.

1. Put the oven on at 190°C / 375°F fan. Peel the squash, and chop that and the beetroot roughly into 2.5cm / 1in squares. Place the squash in a bowl with half the oil and half the thyme. Season, and stir to coat. Spread it out with plenty of room on a baking tray, then do the same with the beetroot on a separate tray. I like to prepare the beetroot and the squash separately so that the squash doesn't take on the red of the beetroot, and it looks more striking when you put it on the table. This is also why I oil the squash first, so I can then use the same bowl for the beetroot. If this doesn't bother you, then feel free to prep and cook the veg together.

2. Place in the oven and cook for 30–40 minutes until the edges are just beginning to brown, turning half way through. If you've crammed it on a baking tray, then it will take longer to brown, so try and use two good-sized baking trays to space it out, and the veg will brown nicely. Depending on what kind of squash you use, and if the beetroot are young or old, the cooking times may vary a little – another reason why it is good to put them on separate trays.

3. I let it cool a little, then add the veg together to a big bowl and crumble the feta cheese on top. Give it a gentle mix to combine, then top with your toasted sunflower seeds to serve.

Serves 4 as a side dish

400g / 14oz purple beetroot
400g / 14oz butternut squash
4 tbsp olive oil
a few sprigs of fresh thyme
150g / 5oz feta cheese
60g / 2oz sunflower
    seeds, toasted

Use what you've grown

Really, any flavoursome orange-fleshed squash will work in this dish. At Homeacres we used Crown Prince squash, which has such a lovely, sweet, nutty flavour. You can try other coloured beetroot if that's what you have, but the earthy taste of the red ones is so good in this. If you don't have thyme, then you can always try using some sage instead. Different, but still good.

Broad bean, pea and feta salad

Being able to make this salad is always a sign for me that we are moving out of the hungry gap and into the fresh and lively flavours of the summer. Simple and so tasty, this is a must-have on any spring picnic, and is always a crowd pleaser.

1. Bring a pot of water to the boil. Shell the broad beans. Add them to the boiling water, and after the water comes back to the boil allow another 3 minutes, then drain and rinse in cold water until cool.

2. De-stem and chop the mint. Add the cooked broad beans and raw sugar snap peas to a suitably sized bowl, with the chopped mint and the lemon juice, and mix well.

3. Crumble in the feta cheese and mix gently.

Serves 4 as a side dish

1kg / 2lb 3oz broad beans in their pods; this should give you about 200g / 6oz of podded beans
200g / 7oz sugar snap peas
100g / 3.5oz feta cheese
small bunch of fresh mint
juice of ½ lemon

Use what you've grown

This recipe is intended for reasonably young broad beans. If there is a black stripe on the beans once you've podded them, then the bean skins might be a bit tough. Personally, I don't like wasting anything that I have grown, but you may want to take the skins off after you have cooked them so you are left only with the tender inner bean. If you are doing this, then you will need to up the amount of beans that you cook.

I love to use podded peas in this recipe too. If you do this, then use double the weight of peas in their pods, as the recipe states the weight of sugar snaps, which should give you the same weight once podded. Add these to boiling water after the broad beans have had a minute. Raw mangetout can also work well in this salad if you have them. Replace weight for weight of sugar snaps. If you don't have peas or mangetout then this works perfectly well with just broad beans (this is the version you see in the photo).

Chard and white bean salad

This is a great salad for the winter months. You can use dried Czar beans, which taste just like butter beans. If you don't grow your own beans, then a tin will do just fine. A great side dish served hot or cold, depending on what you're having it with.

1. Heat the oil in a large frying pan or skillet, then add the onion and cook over a medium heat for 7–8 minutes until soft and translucent but not brown. Add the garlic and cook for another minute, and then add the chard and a splash of water and cook until wilted, about 5 minutes.

2. Add the beans, and the water or stock, and cook for another 5 minutes until the liquid has thickened a little.

3. Turn off the heat and add the grated cheese. Season to taste.

Serves 4–6 as a side dish

4 tbsp olive oil
1 large white onion, finely chopped
5 cloves of garlic
8–12 chard leaves, depending on the size, roughly chopped
450g / 1lb cooked Czar beans (see pp.40–41), or 2 tins drained butter beans
8 tbsp water or vegetable stock
150g / 5oz grated parmesan or other hard cheese
salt and pepper to taste

Use what you've grown

If you have lots of borlotti beans, then feel free to use these instead of Czar, although I think this is better with white beans. Butter beans are a great alternative if you don't have any dried beans.

If you don't have any chard, then spinach or beetroot leaves will do nicely. Even kale can work, but it won't cook down in quite the same way.

Charles's advice on growing your own

Aubergine

Vegetables in the Solanum or nightshade family, including aubergines and potatoes, are mostly fast-growers. However, aubergine plants need warmth at all stages of growth, and I categorise them with melons for their relative growing difficulty in regions with cool summers.

They are not space- or time-efficient, and may give 1.5kg / m² when grown under cover.

Growth is slow: from seed to first harvest is 130 days under cover, to 160 days outside in a temperate climate. Seeds sown in February to mid-March, and grown in warmth under cover, will harvest from July until September.

It stores for 7–10 days at ambient temperature.

Once cooked, the difference in flavour between homegrown and store-bought is not huge.

Broad beans

Broad beans are mostly eaten shelled from their pods when green and fresh. They lose moisture and also sweetness with any lapse of time after picking. Freshly gathered homegrown broad beans have excellent flavour – if you have not eaten them before, do have a try.

They are not difficult to grow and tolerate cool conditions, unlike French and runner beans. They are large plants with a high proportion of leaf and stem compared to the amount of food produced. An approximate yield is 4.5 kg / m², including pods.
- Sowing from mid-October is possible, but the first half of November is better.
- Sow again from February until April.
- It's possible to sow in June and harvest broad beans in late summer and even autumn, but the yield is light compared to the time and space needed.

Seeds sown in late autumn will harvest through early summer. This timing is highly space-efficient, because you can follow them with plantings of anything from beetroot and carrots, to kale and purple sprouting broccoli.

Seeds sown from late winter to mid-spring will harvest through summer.

Pick at any stage of pod and bean size, according to your preference. There is more to eat when you allow pods to swell, and the mature beans inside them can have the skins removed after cooking.

Fennel

Timing is the crucial thing to get right and centres on the same understanding as for kohlrabi: they flower in early to midsummer.

This allows time (just), from a very early sowing, for bulbs to swell before the development of a flower stem inside them. Once a stem initiates, bulbs lose their juicy roundness and become long, thin and fibrous.

Yields are low, around 1kg / m². But they grow quickly and are not difficult or pest-prone.

- Fennel sown in late winter to early spring will have bulbs ready before summer solstice.
- Fennel sown in midsummer, or just after, will have bulbs ready through autumn.

The aniseed flavour is strong, and the texture is good for salads, especially of young bulbs.

In summer, best keep fennel in the fridge, as cool as you can. They stay usable for a week, while losing a little flavour and softness.

Peas

Homegrown peas are a luxury pinnacle of home gardening. Flavour, tenderness, sugar content and bright colour are great reasons to grow your own, especially the fresh sweetness and flavour you notice when snacking during picking!

However, pea plants require an investment of time for growing, supporting, picking, shelling and clearing. An approximate yield is 3kg / m², including pods.

Plants grow best in spring, and offer several harvest options.

- Pea shoots are full of moisture and crop early, while peas in pods have more sugars.
- Some varieties grow pods you can eat, and some have stringy pods with peas you need to shell out.
- Varieties with edible pods are either mangetout, which you harvest when empty of peas, and the pods are quite large, or snap peas which harvest when the pods have sweet peas inside.

Pea plants are hardy to frost and thrive in a damp spring. The standout times to sow are February to March under cover, and March to April outside. This allows plants to capture their natural, healthy time for growing to a decent size, before flowering.

Later sowings encounter the summer season of mildew, and perhaps pea moths too, resulting in smaller harvests. One variety, Terrain, stands out for sowing, even in early July, because of how it resists mildew.

Fennel Perfektion, June

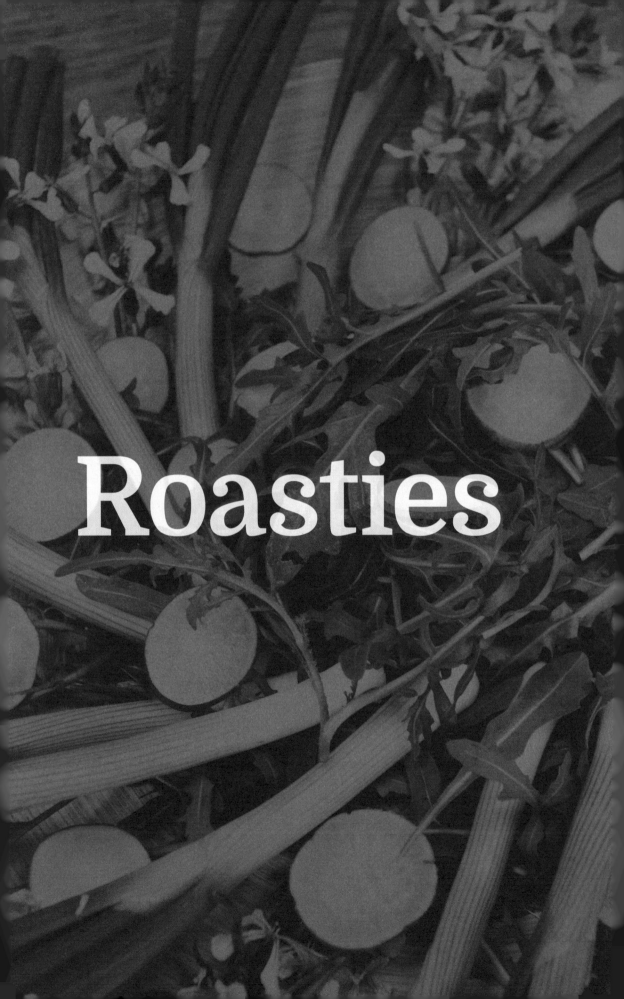

Roasties

Braised spring cabbage and spring onions

Roasted Crown Prince squash

Roasted baby carrots

Cheesy roasted new potatoes

Roasted broccoli and cauliflower with gomashio

Spicy Spanish potatoes

Roasted cauliflower and leeks in cheese sauce

Roasted purple sprouting with tahini dressing

Braised spring cabbage and spring onions

We love roasting most vegetables at Homeacres. Cabbage and onion is a great combination so this is perfect if you have a lot of cabbage to get through, and is a great way to use up any spring onions that have got a bit big. Because of the looseness of a spring cabbage, they won't do so well put straight in the oven, but this recipe keeps the hearts soft and tender, and the outer leaves crisp.

1. Preheat the oven to 180°C / 350°F fan.

2. Cut the cabbage through the stem into 6 wedges, then place in a bowl and rub the oil into the edges of the wedges.

3. Place the cabbage in a roasting dish with enough room that the pieces don't overlap too much, and tuck the onions in between, slicing any larger ones in half. Then scatter the lemon zest and tarragon over the top.

4. Pour over the stock and the vinegar, season generously, cover with foil and bake in the oven for 45 minutes.

5. Remove the wedges from the oven, remove the foil, and carefully turn the wedges over. If the tray is dry, add a little more water. Replace the foil and put them back in the oven for another 45 minutes.

6. Remove the foil and turn the oven up to 200°C / 390°F and roast for another 10 minutes, or until the edges have started to go crispy.

7. Serve immediately with your favourite roast dinner.

Serves 6 as a side dish

1 large head of spring cabbage
4 large spring onions, or more if they are small
3 tbsp olive oil
175ml / ¾ cup vegetable stock
2 tbsp cider vinegar
zest of 1 lemon
2 tbsp tarragon leaves, bruised
salt and pepper

Use what you've grown

You can cook any kind of cabbage in the same way. Spring cabbages are very loose-hearted, so if you're using a cabbage with a tighter heart you will want to extend the cooking time under foil to about 1 hour, or maybe more. You can also use other onions if you haven't got spring onions, just cut them into wedges.

Roasted Crown Prince squash

This is about as simple as it gets, but it looks so lovely all fanned out on a serving plate, and it is such a great-tasting vegetable that your friends will still be impressed.

1. Preheat the oven to 190°C / 375°F fan.

2. Scoop the seeds out of the centre of the squash. Cut it in half, and then cut each half into 6–8 slices. You want each slice to be about 1.5cm / 0.5in thick.

3. Lay them flat onto a baking tray, drizzle with oil and season, then turn them over and do the same on the other side. Place the wedges in the oven for about 40 minutes until they are just starting to brown and blister in places.

4. Using a spatula, take them off the baking tray and arrange on a serving plate. You can either drizzle a little tahini sauce over the top, or put it in a little bowl next to the squash so people can help themselves.

Serves 6–8 as a side dish

½ Crown Prince squash
olive oil
salt and pepper
1 portion of tahini dressing
   (see p.21)

Roasted baby carrots

It almost seems silly to print this recipe as there is really nothing to it, but it is a great thing to do with baby carrots, so here it is. They are just so sweet, and roasting them brings that sweetness out even more.

Don't forget to keep your carrot tops, and use them to make carrot top pesto! (See p.26)

1. Preheat the oven to 190°C / 375°F fan.
2. Scrub your carrots and cut off the tops, leaving the bottom of the stems on. Place in a bowl with the oil and seasoning, and toss to coat.
3. Place onto a baking tray and into the oven for 20–25 minutes until the carrots are tender and starting to brown on the tips.
4. Serve immediately.

Serves 6 as a side dish

700g / 1lb 9oz baby carrots
2 tbsp olive oil
salt and pepper

Cheesy roasted new potatoes

These are great to add a bit of variety to a roast dinner. They are so nice and crispy on the outside and soft on the inside. No matter how many of these I make for a course lunch, there are never any leftovers.

1. Preheat oven to 200°C / 390°F fan.
2. Scrub and cut the potatoes in half, or quarters if they are big. No need to cut baby ones.
3. Place in a large bowl with 80g / 3oz of the cheese and the olive oil. Rub the rosemary sprigs between your hands over the bowl to bruise them and release their aroma, then add them in too, with some seasoning. Toss the potatoes so they are reasonably evenly coated with the oil and cheese.
4. Spread them on a large baking tray, then place in the oven on the top shelf and cook for 40–45 minutes, turning halfway until the cheese is crispy and the potatoes are brown.
5. Take the potatoes out of the oven and sprinkle with the rest of the cheese, then toss to coat and serve immediately.

Serves 6–8 as a side dish

1.5 kg / 3lb 5oz new potatoes
120g / 4oz hard cheese, like parmesan or a hard sheep's cheese
3 sprigs of rosemary
5 tbsp olive oil
salt and pepper

Use what you've grown

If it's not the season for new potatoes, then mature potatoes would also be really tasty cooked like this.

Some dishes for a course lunch, including cheesy roast potatoes; carrot, beetroot and apple salad; and carrot top pesto

Roasted broccoli and cauliflower with gomashio

Cauliflower is my all-time favourite vegetable, and roasting it is probably my preferred way to cook it. It works really well with broccoli, and sprinkling a little gomashio (a simple Japanese condiment often used in macrobiotic cooking) adds a nice little something to the dish, without taking away from the taste of these lovely brassicas.

1. Preheat oven to 180°C / 350°F fan.

2. Cut the cauliflower and broccoli into decent-sized florets and place in a large bowl. Drizzle with the olive oil and season, then toss to coat. Place on a baking tray large enough that there is a little space between your florets so they can brown. Bake for around 25 minutes, turning once. They are done when they are a little brown on the edges but still firm.

Serves 6–8 as a side dish

1 head of cauliflower
1 head of calabrese broccoli
4 tbsp olive oil
salt and pepper
60g / 2oz sesame seeds
1 tsp good quality salt; I prefer Himalayan pink salt for this, but any good salt will do

3. Whilst the veg is roasting, make your gomashio by toasting the sesame seeds in a dry frying pan over a medium heat until they start to pop, stirring all the time so they cook evenly. Remove from the heat and keep stirring for another minute, and then transfer to a bowl to cool.

4. Add the sesame seeds to a spice grinder or mortar and pestle, along with the salt, and grind until they are broken and releasing their oil. They should end up as a coarse powder.

5. When the veggies are cooked, remove from the oven and transfer to a serving plate, then sprinkle with 2–3 tablespoons of the gomashio mix before serving.

6. Once it is cool, transfer the rest of the gomashio into an airtight storage container, a jam jar will do, and store in a cool, dry place for next time. It is also tasty sprinkled over salads or steamed veg.

Spicy Spanish potatoes

Here is my take on patatas bravas. Please excuse me if you are Spanish as I'm sure these are not authentic. However, they still went down really well on the course lunches and taste great.

1. Preheat your oven to 190°C / 375°F.

2. Scrub your potatoes and cut into 2.5cm / 1in chunks.

3. In a small bowl, mix the remaining ingredients (except parsley) together until they form a smooth paste.

4. In a large bowl, combine the potatoes with the tomato and garlic paste until the potatoes are fully coated, then spread onto a large baking tray and place in the top of the oven for 45–50 minutes (turning halfway through), until the potatoes have crisped up around the edges.

5. Transfer to a serving dish, sprinkle with parsley, and serve with a bowl of aioli (see p.21).

Serves 6 as a side dish

1.5kg / 3lb 5oz potatoes
4 tbsp olive oil
3 tbsp tomato puree
6 cloves of garlic, crushed
2 tsp smoked paprika
1 ½ tsp salt
small bunch of parsley,
    de-stemmed and
    roughly chopped

Spicy Spanish potatoes with aioli

Roasted cauliflower and leeks in cheese sauce

This is just the best comfort food, in my opinion. Roasting the veg makes it way more tasty, and using oat milk in the cheese sauce means it's much less rich than you would expect, without taking anything away from this classic dish.

1. Preheat the oven to 180°C / 350°F fan and spread the cauliflower florets and the leeks onto a baking dish big enough that they fit snugly in an even layer. Season and drizzle with the oil, giving a little toss to coat, and bake for about 20 minutes until the cauliflower is starting to brown around the edges.

2. While the veggies are cooking, make your cheese sauce by melting the butter in a saucepan then adding the flour, and cook, stirring for 2 minutes. Then add the milk a little at a time, stirring constantly and making sure the sauce is smooth before you add more milk. This will prevent you getting a lumpy sauce. If you're worried about lumps, then you can use a whisk to get it smooth again. Once all the milk has been added, cook for another 3–4 minutes until the sauce has thickened, then add the mustard and stir well. Add two thirds of the cheese, and stir until it has completely melted into the sauce.

3. When the veggies are ready, remove from the oven and pour the sauce over the top. Sprinkle with the rest of the cheese and put the dish back in the oven for another 10–15 minutes until the cheese has melted and it is starting to brown.

4. Serve immediately with crusty bread or roast potatoes and some steamed greens.

Serves 4 as a main course or 6 as a side dish

1 large cauliflower, cut into large florets
3 leeks, washed well and sliced into 2.5cm / 1in rings
1 tbsp olive oil
2 tbsp plain flour
30g / 1oz butter
250ml / 1 cup oat milk
3 tbsp wholegrain mustard
75g / 2.5oz cheddar cheese

Use what you've grown
You can always use broccoli instead of the leeks, or even onions cut into wedges. You can always have cauliflower as the only veg if you like, simple and classic.

Roasted purple sprouting with tahini dressing

You wouldn't think that purple sprouting lends itself well to roasting, but surprisingly it does. While the florets stay soft in the middle, any leaves go really nice and crispy, which is such a great combination of textures. A great way to use up a glut of this delicious brassica.

1. Preheat the oven to 200°C / 390°F fan.

2. Go though the sprouting florets and put a cut down the middle of any very thick stems so they cook through.

3. Place all the ingredients, apart from the tahini dressing, in a bowl, and mix well using your hands, making sure to rub the oil into the leaves.

4. Spread the purple sprouting out on a baking tray, and place on the top shelf of the oven for 10–12 minutes until the leaves are crispy and the florets are just starting to go brown.

5. While the broccoli is in the oven, add a tablespoon of water to the tahini dressing to thin it out a little, and mix well.

6. Remove the purple sprouting from the oven and transfer to a serving dish, then drizzle with the tahini dressing.

Serves 4–6 as a side dish

450g / 1lb purple sprouting
2 tbsp olive oil
a pinch of chilli flakes
zest of 1 lemon
salt and pepper
2 tbsp of tahini dressing
   (see p.21)

Use what you've grown
You can use any kind of broccoli sprouting for this recipe. You are looking for finger-width stems with a few leaves still on, to give you that great mix of textures.

Charles's advice on growing your own

Broccoli

The name covers green calabrese in summer and autumn, as well as purple sprouting broccoli for harvests in late winter and until mid-spring.

Homegrown broccoli's sweet and tender stems have amazing flavours. Plants grow readily in cool and warmer climates, and from one sowing you can harvest up to 3kg / m² over a month or more.

Calabrese can mature in 100–120 days from seed to harvest, compared to 170–300 for sprouting broccoli.

- Sow from late February to early July, harvest from June to November for calabrese.
- Sow from January to May for sprouting broccoli.

Pick when the buds are differentiating and before any sign of flowering. Younger shoots have tender stems which are perhaps the best bit, akin to asparagus.

Broccoli stores best in the fridge, but for a few days only. It's best picked fresh. In cool weather, there is less rush to harvest so in winter months, pick your moment to pick!

Cauliflower

Plants need much space for the results we desire, and need fertile soil plus temperate weather. They pose a challenge, but it's worth it for harvests of great flavour, colour and beauty. When you succeed, you know you are a good gardener.

An approximate yield is 2 kg / m².

First sowings are from mid-February under cover, through spring and summer. Last sowings can even be in October, to grow under cover as transplants for spring. There is a mass of possibilities, and check the seed packet details to make sure you're growing a correct variety, for the harvest period you want.

- Cauliflower sown in late winter will harvest in early to midsummer.
- Cauliflower sown in late spring to early summer will harvest through autumn.
- Cauliflower sown in mid- to late summer will harvest in early to mid-spring.

Watch for the curds developing; they are barely visible at first, and were nicer when young. If they were very mature and perhaps a little discoloured when you cut them, they are then best eaten within two to three days, because some decay is probably already happening.

At temperatures below 10°C / 50°F, cauliflowers may store for up to a week.

Leeks

A flavour for three seasons at least, sweet and welcome in many dishes. They are not difficult to grow, unless your soil is contaminated with allium leaf miner, a difficult pest.

The summer transplant time makes leeks a wonderful succession vegetable. Pop them in after any summer harvests such as potatoes, beetroot etc.

An approximate yield of 3.5kg / m² is not huge, but has extra value because leeks are so hardy to cold. You have a long harvest season from any one planting.

The best sowing time is early to mid-April. Earlier sowing is possible, for summer harvests, but there is some risk of bolting. People who sow early can make you feel that you missed the boat! This is terrible because with leeks, you can sow as late as May, especially varieties such as Bandit, whose harvest period is March to early May.

- Leeks of summer and autumn varieties, sown in March, give harvests in late summer through autumn.
- Leeks of autumn and winter varieties, sown mainly in April, give harvests from late autumn until spring.

Leeks stand well in the ground outside, or you could store them for two months after a harvest with roots on, kept in a container or bucket in the shed. Or trim the roots at harvest and keep them in a garage or shed, where they stay good for two weeks.

Potatoes

Growth is fast, potatoes are easy to harvest, they store well and give a lot of food per area. Second earlies harvested mid-July can give 6kg / m², and you still have time after their harvest to grow another vegetable.

Homegrown potatoes have a richer flavour than bought ones, especially when new but even when older as well. Flavour reflects the soil they grew in, as well as which variety they are, and there is a wonderful choice to tempt you.

When buying seed potatoes, check that you know which type they are – first early, second early or maincrop. The harvest period for all three types together is around four months, between June and first frost. The total eating period is most of the year, because potatoes store so well in two-ply paper sacks.

- First earlies planted from late March to mid-April are ready by June.
- Second earlies planted in April are ready by the end of July.
- Maincrops planted by mid-May are ready by or before September.

I do not recommend summer plantings, whose harvests are small because they are growing out of season.

The key factor in deciding when to plant is your last frost date. You need to know this average date for your area, and pop in seed potatoes three to four weeks before it.

Squash (winter / Crown Prince)

Squash can give a bountiful harvest of excellent flavour which stores for several months. Plants are easy to grow when summer temperatures are 21°C / 70°F or more in the afternoons. Each one needs a square metre to grow, and from that you can pick up to 10 kg / m² of sweet fruits, which store really well.

You have much choice of variety. Easiest are red Kuri types for harvests by early September, with small fruits of 1–2kg / 2–4lb which store until March. Crown Prince weigh 3–4kg / 7–9lb and have a top flavour, along with Marina di Chioggia. Butternut types need a long time to grow, and are best where warm summers allow time for their skins to harden by mid-October.

- Sow no earlier than 3–4 weeks before your last frost date. This allows time to raise a large plant, and gains a month of growing time. At Homeacres, we sow from 15–25 April, to transplant by the end of May.

The harvest is from mid-September until first frost, and then keep squash in the house so they stay warm and dry, to finish hardening the skin. You can keep them in the house all winter and through spring: the hard skin means they retain moisture, and the flavour sweetens over time.

I find it amazing that some of the Crown Prince, in particular, and butternut types if you got them ripe, are still excellent to eat as late as June. They are a great vegetable for the hungry gap, more than a half year after harvest.

Opposite above: Second early potatoes in late June, which we harvested three weeks later

Opposite below: The same beds in early September, with July plantings of endive, lettuce, kale and leeks

Stews
and
hot
dishes

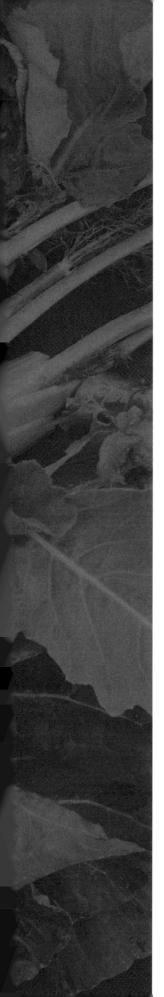

Beetroot curry

Celeriac gratin

Chard bhajis

Crown Prince and spinach stew

Dandelion flower fritters

Fried aubergine, green pepper and tomatoes

Garlic beans

Herby braised radishes

Honey-glazed turnips

Italian bean and kale stew – Ribollita

Turkish borlotti bean stew – Barbunya Pilaki

Beetroot curry

I spent a couple of years living in South India, and the food was just amazing. The flavours were always so fresh, the vegetables in the curries were crispy (just cooked enough but never too much), and the amazing smell of coconut oil, curry leaves and mustard seeds was often in the air. Cooking this curry, and the smells it releases, reminds me fondly of that time and the great food I ate there. It is also a great and different thing to do with beetroot, something that there always seems to be an abundance of in the Homeacres garden.

Serves 4 as a main course

3 tbsp coconut oil
2 tsp black mustard seeds
½ tsp cumin seeds
15 curry leaves; fresh ones are available from a good Asian supermarket, but you can get dried from most big supermarkets
¼ tsp ground cinnamon
1 green chilli, de-seeded and chopped (keep the seeds in if you like things spicy)
1 large onion, chopped
2 cloves of garlic, crushed
½ tsp turmeric powder
750g /1lb 10oz red beetroot
½ tsp salt
200g / 7oz fresh tomatoes, chopped; tinned will do if you don't have fresh
juice of 1 lime
1 tbsp fresh coriander, chopped

1. Cut the beetroot into batons about 1cm / 0.5in thick. It doesn't matter if they are a little smaller, but I wouldn't go bigger than that or they won't cook quickly.

2. Heat the oil in a large, deep frying pan, then add the mustard seeds, cumin seeds, curry leaves and cinnamon, and heat until the spices release their flavour and start to pop.

3. Add the onion and chilli, with or without seeds, and fry for 3–4 minutes. Then add the garlic and cook for a couple of minutes more, or until the onion is soft and cooked through.

4. Stir in the turmeric, then the beetroot and tomatoes, and add the salt. Cover and cook over a medium heat for 10 minutes, stirring once or twice, making sure it doesn't stick.

5. Remove the lid, and give it a stir. If it is dry and sticking to the pan, then add a little water. Replace the lid and cook for a further 5 minutes.

6. Your veggies should be cooked through but still crunchy. Turn off the heat, add the lime juice, and scatter the coriander over the top, then serve immediately with rice or chapati.

Use what you've grown

You can replace some of the beetroot with dwarf or runner beans, or even some kale, or other green leaves if you are lacking in beetroot. If using dwarf beans or kale add them on step 5. They don't need as long as the beetroot to cook. Beetroot and dwarf beans make a lovely combination. My recommendation is to replace a third of the beetroot with the same weight of beans. If you use kale then maybe only a quarter kale and three quarters beetroot.

Celeriac gratin

So many people said to me this year, 'I don't like celeriac, but I really like this', and to be honest this did include me too. Celeriac has a lovely flavour when you work out how to combine it with other things that will complement and soften it. I love growing it, and always have more than I can use when only including it as a tiny ingredient in a bigger dish. However, in this recipe it is the main event, and totally delicious. You'll notice that I don't use cow's milk or cream in this, as you might expect in a gratin. This is simply because I find that these things create a very rich dish, whereas I prefer a slightly more simple taste, and it also means I can eat more of it without feeling like I've overdone it!

If you want to make this vegan, then replace the butter with oil and use yeast flakes or a nut cheese instead of cheddar.

1. In a large pan, melt the butter and add the leeks, thyme and bay leaf, and then cook over a medium heat, stirring regularly for 10–15 minutes until the leeks are soft. Then add the garlic and cook for 5 minutes more.

2. Add the oat milk and some seasoning to the pan and bring to the boil, then turn off and leave to cool a little.

3. Preheat the oven to 180°C / 350°F fan. Spoon a little of the leek and milk mix into an ovenproof dish, and then arrange a layer of celeriac over the top. Spoon over a little more of the leeks and milk, and then sprinkle with a little cheese. Repeat this process until all the leeks and celeriac have been used up, and finish with the remaining cheese, making sure that all the celeriac is covered, or it will go dry in the oven.

4. Bake for about 1hr-1hr 15 minutes until the celeriac is cooked. You can test this by inserting a knife into the middle of the gratin.

5. Bring it out of the oven and scatter with some chopped fresh parsley.

Serves 4–8, depending on whether its a main or a side

30g / 1oz butter
2 leeks, well washed and sliced into rings
3 cloves of garlic, crushed
1 celeriac (about 600g / 1lb 5oz), peeled, halved and sliced into 3–5mm slices
a sprig of thyme
450ml / 2 cups oat milk
100g / 3.5oz cheddar cheese
chopped parsley to serve

Use what you've grown

This gratin also works really well using squash instead of celeriac. In the photo opposite, it's made with Crown Prince squash. If you use squash, then add 8–10 sage leaves to the leeks instead of the thyme. Everything else is exactly the same.

Chard bhajis

This recipe was given to me by my allotment neighbours, Nick and Jane, during a chat over the dividing path about what you can do with chard. Chard has a strong, earthy taste and so lends itself well to this recipe. You don't lose the flavour amongst the batter and the deep frying. These have been a massive hit at the Homeacres lunches with the guests and staff alike. Well done Nick for thinking this one up, and thanks for letting me share it.

Makes 8 bhajis

1 onion
2–4 chard leaves, depending on the size
100g / 3.5oz gram flour
½ tsp baking powder
½ tsp turmeric
1 tsp ground cumin
1 green chilli, de-seeded and chopped (optional)
vegetable oil for frying

1. Sift the flour, baking powder and dried spices into a bowl. Then add the chopped chilli (if using) and a good pinch of salt. Add 100ml / ½ cup of water to make a thick batter. Add the water slowly, making sure that the batter is not too runny. You can always add more if it seems too thick.

2. Chop the onion in half and then finely slice it into half rings. Chop the chard and the stems into bite-sized pieces and mix together with the onions in a bowl.

3. Add the batter to the bowl with the chard and onions and mix well. The batter should coat the vegetables easily.

4. Heat about 5cm / 2in of veg oil in a deep pan or wok. To test if it's hot enough, drop a small blob of batter into the oil. If it rises to the surface, bubbling, then it is ready.

5. This is where it gets messy. You can use two spoons if you like, but I find it easier to use my hands. Using a spoon, pick up a spoonful of batter, and, with your other hand, try to mould it into a rough ball shape, then drop it in the batter. Do this a few times, cooking for around 4–5 minutes, and turning the bhajis halfway through the cooking time. They should be lightly brown on both sides.

6. Remove from the oil with a slotted spoon and place on kitchen paper to drain. Keep them warm while you cook the rest.

7. Serve, and then bask in the praise from your friends or family!

Use what you've grown
If you don't have chard, you can always try using leaf beet, spinach, or even beetroot leaves.

Chard bhajis

Dandelion flower fritters

These little treasures brighten up any spring dinner table, and they taste just delicious. All parts of the dandelion are edible, and they are incredibly rich in vitamins and minerals. A real treat for the hungry gap.

When you pick your dandelion flowers, make sure you don't ever take more than you need, and always think about leaving some for the bees. These flowers are their only source of food in the early spring.

1. Pick your flowers just before you need them, as once picked, they will slowly start to close up. You can't really wash them as they won't fry well when wet, so inspect them for little creatures, leave them flower-side down on some paper, and give them a tap to encourage any little friends to move on.

2. Make your batter by sieving the flours into a large bowl, and mix in the salt. Gently mix in your water and the ice, being careful to not beat the bubbles out of the water. They help to give you a lovely, light batter.

3. Add about 3cm / 1in of oil to a deep, wide pan or frying pan, and heat until a drop of batter rises to the top surrounded by bubbles.

4. While the oil is heating up, add your flowers to the batter, and mix in gently so the flowers are covered.

Makes 30 fritters, enough for 4–6 as a side dish

30 dandelion heads
60g / 2oz cornflour
40g / 1.4oz plain flour
½ tsp salt
80ml / ⅓ cup sparkling water, ice cold; I pop it in the freezer just for 30 minutes before I use it
2 crushed ice cubes
vegetable oil for frying

Use what you've grown

You can use this batter recipe and fry lots of different things. Courgette or any squash flowers are really tasty done in this way, and look stunning as a side dish. Broccoli or cauliflower florets also work really well: just make sure they are not too big so they can cook through quickly. You can get really adventurous with this, and pretty much try battering and frying whatever you fancy. Things that wouldn't work very well would be anything that's naturally wet or has a super smooth skin, like a tomato.

5. One at a time, pick out the flowers and drop them into the hot oil. Depending on the size of your pan, you might have to do this in two batches. Give them about 2 minutes and then turn them. They should be slightly golden. Fry them for another 2 minutes and then, using a slotted spoon, remove them onto some kitchen paper to drain.

6. Put them in a serving dish and lightly sprinkle with a little salt, then serve immediately.

Crown Prince and spinach stew

This is a great winter-warmer stew. When I started to make this in the winter it was too early for celery in the garden so I made it without. It is a better flavour with, but still great if you don't have it. The same goes for the carrots. If you still have squash by the time tomato season comes round, then replace the tinned tomatoes with fresh.

1. Heat the oil in a large saucepan, and fry your onion, garlic, carrots and celery on a medium heat for 7–8 minutes until the onion is cooked but not brown.

2. Add your tinned tomatoes, stock, bay leaf and thyme, bring to the boil, then reduce and simmer with the lid on for 45 minutes. If you are using fresh tomatoes, then reduce this cooking time to 20 minutes.

3. Add the squash, replace the lid and cook for a further 15–20 minutes until the squash is cooked through. Then add the spinach and the marjoram, and cook for a couple of minutes more until the spinach is wilted. Season with salt and pepper to taste, and serve with crusty bread or a tasty wholegrain of your choice.

Serves 4 as a main dish

2 tbsp olive oil
1 large onion, chopped
4 cloves of garlic, crushed
2 carrots, finely chopped
2 sticks celery, finely chopped
1 bay leaf
3–4 sprigs of fresh thyme
2 tins chopped tomatoes or 8 plump fresh tomatoes, skinned and chopped
300ml / 1 ¼ cups veg or chicken stock
800g / 1lb 12oz Crown Prince, de-seeded, peeled and chopped in 2cm / 1 in cubes
300g / 11 oz spinach, roughly chopped, or not if they are baby leaves
2 tbsp fresh marjoram

Use what you've grown

You can use butternut squash or pumpkin instead of the Crown Prince, and chard instead of spinach if that's what you have. This changes the flavour a little, as chard is an earthier flavour, and if using it to replace the spinach, I would be inclined to use slightly less weight so it doesn't dominate the dish. Try 200g / 7oz instead.

Aubergines De Barbentane in polytunnel, August

Fried aubergine, green pepper and tomatoes

This is another stunner of a dish. It is a great simple recipe to show off the flavours of your homegrown Mediterranean veg.

1. Slice the aubergine into 1.5cm / 0.5in rounds, and spread out on a baking sheet. Sprinkle both sides generously with salt, and leave for 30–45 minutes. This brings out the bitter juices from the aubergine so you get a better flavour.

2. Pat the aubergine slices dry and heat 3 tbsp oil in a frying pan. You want the oil nice and hot so the aubergine doesn't soak it up, but not so hot that the oil starts to smoke. Fry on each side for 3–4 minutes until just golden brown. Remove from the pan and put on kitchen paper.

3. While your aubergine is frying, de-seed and cut your peppers into six or eight wedges. Add another 2 tbsp of oil to the pan, and when it's hot, fry your pepper skin-side down for 2–3 minutes until the skin is brown and blistered. Remove from the pan and place on the kitchen paper to drain.

4. While the pepper is cooking, slice the beefy tomatoes horizontally into 1.5cm / 0.5in slices and then slice the garlic.

5. If needed, add the remaining oil to the pan. When hot, add the tomatoes and fry for 2–3 minutes on one side, then turn them and add the garlic, and fry for another 2–3 minutes.

6. While your tomatoes are cooking, arrange a layer of aubergines on a serving plate and sprinkle with a little of the sumac, then add the peppers and sprinkle with a little more sumac. Then, using a slotted spoon, remove the tomatoes and layer them on top of your peppers. Sprinkle with the rest of the sumac. De-stem and roughly chop the parsley, and scatter on top.

Serves 4 as a side dish

1 large aubergine
good quality salt
6 tbsp extra virgin olive oil
2 large green peppers
4 beef or large tomatoes
6 cloves of garlic
2 tsp sumac
small bunch fresh parsley

Use what you've grown

Obviously we can't deviate too dramatically from the veggies listed in the recipe, but if you don't have green peppers use whatever colour you do have, and if you haven't grown big beefy tomatoes, then plum tomatoes work well. Just cut these in half vertically. You can try using normal-sized tomatoes and cut these in half vertically too. The issue with these types of tomatoes is that they have a lot more seeds in them than beefy types or plum that will likely come out in the frying pan, so you may want to de-seed them before frying.

Garlic beans

You don't need to do much, if anything, to a green bean to make them taste great. I love to eat them raw when they are young. When they get a bit bigger this is super quick, easy, and really tasty. You will be able to munch through that glut of beans in no time.

1. Top and tail the beans. Put a steamer over a pan of boiling water, and then steam your beans for 3–4 minutes. They don't need long. You want the beans to still be bright and firm with a nice crunch.

2. Turn off the heat and take the steamer off the pan. Empty the water and then put your beans back into the warm pan. Add the butter and the garlic, and stir until the butter is melted and the beans are coated.

3. Serve immediately.

Serves 4 as a side dish

500g / 1lb dwarf beans
3 tbsp butter
2–4 cloves of garlic, depending on how much you like garlic, crushed

Use what you've grown

This works with runner beans too, or most greens. A sweet cabbage, sliced thinly, is also lovely like this, as is curly kale.

Herby braised radishes

Well, who would have thought that radishes tasted so good cooked? It was a new one to me, that's for certain. I love a raw radish with my salad, and I don't know about you, but no matter how hard I try to stagger my radish plantings, I always end up with too many to eat at one time, before some of them go past their best. When they get big and really peppery, this dish is a great way to eat them, and uses up a good bunch at once so you can keep up with your radish harvest.

1. Add the olive oil and butter to a large frying pan on a medium heat, then add the radishes to the pan and fry for 10 minutes.
2. Add the herbs and fry for another 2 minutes.
3. Add the vinegar and the salt and pepper, and fry for another minute, then remove from the heat and serve immediately.

Serves 6 as a side dish

800g / 1lb 12oz salad radishes, bigger ones halved or quartered
1 tbsp olive oil
3 tbsp unsalted butter
large bunch of fresh mixed herbs; tarragon, dill and parsley is a good combination
1 tbsp red wine vinegar
salt and pepper to taste

Use what you've grown

You can explore using different herbs. Mint and dill also go well together, but you can try thyme and sage, or any combination that takes your fancy or is available in the garden.

Honey-glazed turnips

Before I started working with Charles, it had never occurred to me to eat baby turnips. I always used them fully grown as a tasty addition to soups and stews. The first very tiny ones we ate raw, which were delicious, but once they were a bit big for that but still tender and young, this seemed a great way to show off their lovely flavour.

1. Place your turnips in a large frying pan with the butter, honey, thyme and water. Cover with a lid and bring to the boil, then keep on a high simmer for 10 minutes.

2. Uncover and turn up the heat slightly to keep on a boil for another 10 minutes, or until nearly all the liquid has evaporated.

3. Add the lemon juice and serve.

Serves 4 as a side dish

700g / 1lb 9oz baby turnips
50g / 1.7oz unsalted butter
3 tbsp honey
a few sprigs of fresh thyme
1 tbsp lemon juice
200ml / ¾ cup water

Italian bean and kale stew – Ribollita

This is a little more complicated, as it has a longer ingredients list than many recipes in this book, but it is worth the effort. Usually ribollita is made with crusty stale bread included in the stew, but I have left that out as we are always focused on the vegetables here at Homeacres. I really enjoy Mediterranean food. The herbs, tomatoes and cheese are always a winner for me, and this recipe is a great combination of all of the above, plus it has beans as the star of the show. You can't go wrong!

1. Heat the olive oil in a large, heavy-based pan, and cook the onion, celery and carrots for 10–12 minutes over a medium heat until soft. Add the garlic and the chilli flakes and cook for 1 minute more.

2. Add the tomatoes, stock, rosemary, thyme, bay leaf and parmesan rind, and cook for 25 minutes.

3. Then add the kale and the beans and cook for another 5 minutes or so until the kale is wilted and the beans are hot through.

4. Season your stew and serve with the grated parmesan and crusty bread.

Serves 4 as a main dish

3 tbsp olive oil
1 large onion, chopped
2 celery sticks, finely chopped
2 medium carrots, diced small
4 cloves of garlic, crushed
a pinch of chilli flakes (optional)
400g / 14oz fresh tomatoes, peeled and chopped, or 1 tin chopped tomatoes
1 sprig rosemary
2 sprigs thyme
1 bay leaf
500ml / 2 cups vegetable stock
Continued on next page

250g / 9oz cooked Czar beans
(see p.41), or 1 tin of
white beans, drained
1 parmesan rind
350g / 12oz cavolo nero, chopped
grated parmesan to serve
(optional)

Use what you've grown

I have made this before with borlotti beans and chard instead of white beans and kale and it was really good. Any green leaf will work with this – curly or red kale could be good or even spinach. And don't worry if you don't have a parmesan rind, it will be okay without it.

Turkish borlotti bean stew – Barbunya Pilaki

I love growing borlotti beans, partly because I can store them dry and use them throughout the winter, so no need for freezer or fridge space. When I started cooking at Homeacres, I was so pleased to discover that Charles grows enough for me to feature them in almost every course lunch through the year, which is a lot! This meant I could really explore the possibilities of cooking with these yummy and beautiful beans. This simple Turkish recipe is really all about the beans, so you can fully experience the joy of the borlotti.

1. Heat the oil in a thick-bottomed pan and add the onions. Cook for about 5 minutes until the onion is soft, then add the carrots and garlic and cook for another 2 minutes.

2. Add the chopped tomatoes and 120ml / ½ cup of water and cook for 20 minutes. Then add a little more water and the beans, and cover and cook for another 20–30 minutes, adding more water if you want more or thinner sauce. You want the beans to be cooked but not mushy.

3. Take off the heat and add the parsley, then serve with lemon wedges.

Serves 6 as a main dish

700g / 1lb 9oz cooked borlotti
beans (see p.40)
3 tbsp olive oil
1 large onion
3 medium-sized carrots, cut
into small dice
3 cloves of garlic, crushed
400g / 14oz fresh tomatoes,
peeled and chopped, or 1 tin
of chopped tomatoes
240ml / 1 cup water
small bunch of parsley, chopped
1 lemon, cut into wedges

Use what you've grown

You can do this with fresh borlotti beans. You will need about 1kg / 2lb 3oz of beans in their pods to give you about 700g / 1lb 9oz of podded beans. You can also use fresh or dried Czar beans. If you don't have your own beans, then you can always use tinned beans. You need the drained weight to be 700g / 1lb 9oz.

Charles's advice on growing your own

Chard

The flavour of chard is not as amazing as spinach, in my view. There is a metallic edge, perhaps from the high iron content.

However, chard's harvest season from summer to late autumn very nicely complements the season of true spinach, which harvests from autumn to late spring. Plus there are amazing colours to enjoy, and the crunchy stems.

A key understanding is that chard flowers in early spring. Therefore, if you sow too early in spring, there is a risk of flower stems before the plants are very old.

Chard sown in mid-spring is ready to harvest from midsummer and may continue into next spring.

Chard sown in early summer gives harvests through autumn, and is more likely to survive winter, compared to earlier sowings.

Pick leaves small or large, for use in salads or to cook. Larger leaves weigh a lot and this is a space-efficient vegetable, giving up to 7kg / m².

In a polythene bag in cool temperatures, chard can store in nice condition for up to ten days.

Kale

Homegrown kale has strong flavour and excellent nutrition. Vitamins C and K, for example, are at a maximum in fresh leaves, which also boast 3% protein. A long season of regular harvests can result in yields of 4kg / m².

Choose a sowing time according to the size of the leaves you desire and when you want them. Sowing commences in March and stays possible at any time through the following six months.

- Sowings before April give kale through summer, with leaves quite large, and less tender in dry conditions. Harvests reduce through autumn but can continue into the following spring, if the winter is mild.
- Sowings in mid-May to June give abundant leaves from late summer, through autumn, and then probably until spring.
- Late summer sowings are good for 22cm / 9in spacing to give small leaves, excellent in winter salads. They are especially worth growing under cover, for more harvests in winter.

Ruby and Peppermint chard

Kale cavolo nero and Dazzling Blue

Kale's best harvest season is in the cooler months, when there are fewer insects, and the green leaves are so welcome. In spring, the harvests of flowering shoots, like small broccoli, have sweet stems.

Kale turns yellow after picking unless kept cool, below about 10°C / 50°F. A little water on leaves, in a polythene bag, helps them store well.

Radish

Radish are amazing in April and May, when the cooler conditions result in a mild and less pungent flavour. Their harvest is the first root vegetable of spring, closely followed by turnips.

- For red globe radish, multisow under cover in February to April, and from March directly outside. Later sowings encounter more pests such as flea beetles.
- Sow in early September for nice harvests after mid-October.

- For large winter radish, sow in the second half of July. These come ready to harvest in autumn and should survive winter outside, although by February the quality is reduced.

Winter radish are great both in salads and stir fried. They have crisp texture and sometimes beautiful colours, such as the Green Luobo.

Spinach

Eating season for true spinach, as opposed to beet leaves ('perpetual spinach'), is October until mid-June. Plants resist temperatures down to -15°C / 5°F, giving up to 4kg / m² of leaves.

Spinach is a delicious, reliable and efficient plant to have in your garden for repeat picking, excellent to eat both raw and cooked. I love it raw, as part of a mixed salad. A bonus is how, during cold weather, the leaves turn noticeably sweeter. By early spring, in particular, some leaves can be sugary.

- The best time to sow is late summer, and from that one sowing you can enjoy up to eight months of picking leaves.
- Sow also under cover from February until early April, for harvests throughout spring.

Once spinach sends up a flowering stem, its time of leaf production is over. Twist out the plants to compost, and wait for the next sowing time to start again.

Turnips

I recommend the newer type of Japanese or hakurei turnip. They are sweeter, smaller and have delicious, tender leaves. Try a variety such as Tokyo Cross F1, and you will notice they are sweeter and denser than older varieties.

There are two sowing times – very early in late winter, and then in August, as high summer finishes. In between these times is when turnips flower, with woody roots.

- Multisow under cover in mid-February, to transplant outside by the end of March, with fleece over. You then have very welcome harvests of early and sweet roots during the hungry gap. Harvest small for best flavour, because they go somewhat woody by the end of May.
- Multisow again in August's second week, for harvests through October and November. I grow these under a mesh cover, against flea beetles eating leaves and then root fly maggots damaging the turnips.

Traditional turnips are more watery and do not store as well as swedes. They contain cyanoglocosides, which some people's taste buds react badly to. If that's you, try the Japanese type.

6th September – teepees of borlotti for dry beans, with Zinnia elegans in front and an August planting of lettuce on the right

Sweet
treats

Courgette cookies

I don't think I know anyone who grows courgettes and doesn't have too many of them at some point in the summer. I am no exception, and I'm always looking for new and interesting ways to use these versatile vegetables. They work well in cake, giving these cookies a lovely moistness and flavour. No one would ever know there are courgettes in them from the taste, and if you use yellow courgettes, they just look like normal chocolate chip cookies so you can fool those that are not convinced by vegetables in pudding. I like to make mine with a xylitol (sugar substitute made from birch tree sap) and sugar-free chocolate so I can eat them in abundance without guilt, but replace it with the same weight of sugar if you prefer.

If you are not a fan of chocolate chips then sultanas work really well as a substitute.

1. Preheat the oven to 175°C / 350°F fan.

2. Sift the flour, cinnamon, bicarbonate of soda and salt into a bowl, add the oats and mix well.

3. In a large bowl, mix the butter and xylitol (or sugar) together until light and fluffy, then add the egg, vanilla and grated courgette and mix well.

Makes about 20 cookies

250g / 9oz plain flour
1 tsp cinnamon
½ tsp bicarbonate of soda
¼ tsp salt
100g / 3.5oz oats
115g / 4oz butter
Continued on next page

4. Add the dry ingredients to the wet and stir until combined, then fold in the chocolate chips.

5. Lightly grease a baking tray and place heaped dessert spoonfuls of the mixture onto the tray, leaving enough room in between for the cookies to spread out. Bake the cookies for 12–15 minutes until golden brown on top. Leave to cool on the baking tray for a few minutes before placing them on a rack to cool completely.

170g / 6oz xylitol or sugar
1 large egg
1 tsp vanilla essence
200g / 7oz courgettes, grated
170g / 6oz chocolate chips

Raspberry and white chocolate cookies

With this combination you can't go wrong, but I am a massive fan of raspberries so I am completely biased. When I started cooking on the no dig courses, this was one of the first recipes I was asked for, so it seems only right for it to be included in the book, as this collection was put together in response to so many course attendees requesting recipes.

1. Preheat the oven to 190°C / 375°F fan and lightly grease two large baking trays.

2. Place the butter and sugars in a mixing bowl and mix together until light and fluffy, then add the egg and lemon zest and mix these in too.

3. Sift in the flour, salt and bicarbonate of soda, and mix until well combined. Then add the white chocolate chips and stir to mix.

4. Add the raspberries and very gently mix these in. Some will crush and bleed into the mix and some pieces will hopefully stay more intact.

5. The mix will make around 20 cookies, depending on how big you make them. Start with half the dough and divide into about 10 dough balls, about 1½ tbsp for each ball. Place them on the trays, well spaced so they can spread, and flatten them slightly with your fingers.

6. Bake the cookies for about 15 minutes until they are starting to brown slightly around the edges. Remove from the oven and leave to cool for 10 minutes before transferring to a wire rack.

Makes 20 cookies

140g / 5oz butter, softened
70g / 2.5oz soft light
    brown sugar
75g / 2.5oz white sugar
1 large egg
zest of 1 lemon
225g / 8oz plain flour
¾ tsp bicarbonate of soda
¾ tsp salt
85g / 3oz fresh raspberries
100g / 3.5oz white
    chocolate chips

Carrot muffins with mascarpone cheese icing

Carrot muffins with mascarpone cheese icing

Carrot cake is probably my favourite cake and always has been. The carrots make it so moist and then the cream cheese icing is just a dreamy topping for an already pretty dreamy cake. These mini muffin versions always go down a treat on course days. Although you can't actually taste the carrots, they wouldn't taste the same without them.

1. Preheat the oven to 180°C / 350°F fan and line a muffin tray with 12 muffin cases.

2. Combine the carrots, butter and sugar in a bowl and mix well.

3. Sift in the flour, spices and baking powder and mix roughly.

4. Add the beaten eggs, sultanas and chopped nuts and stir to combine.

5. Divide equally between the 12 muffin cases and bake for 20 minutes, or until a skewer inserted into the centre of a muffin comes out clean.

6. Make your icing by sifting the icing sugar into a bowl and adding the remaining ingredients, then mixing well.

7. When the muffins are completely cool, top with the mascarpone icing, sprinkling over a few extra chopped walnuts or some orange zest to decorate if you wish.

Makes 12 muffins

For the muffins
150g / 5oz butter, softened
250g / 9oz carrots, grated
200g / 7oz sugar
200g / 7oz flour
1½ tsp ground cinnamon
¼ tsp ground nutmeg
2 tsp baking powder
2 large eggs, beaten
140g / 5oz sultanas
60g / 2oz walnuts, chopped

For the icing
250g / 9oz mascarpone cheese
2 tsp vanilla extract
2 tbsp icing sugar
1 tbsp orange juice (optional)

Apple and sultana muffins

*A classic combination offered in muffin form. These are the cakes I make
for the courses in the very early spring, using the last of the apples that
have been kept from the previous autumn. It is a great way to use up
apples that you've kept over winter, that are by now a bit too wrinkly
and soft to be eaten just as they are.*

1. Preheat the oven to 180°C / 350°F fan, and place
    12 paper muffin cases in a muffin tray.

2. In a large bowl, mix the flour, baking powder,
    cinnamon and sugar.

3. In a separate bowl, mix the eggs, milk and oil
    together, and stir to combine. Then stir in the
    grated apple and sultanas.

4. Add the wet ingredients to the dry and mix roughly.
    Then divide the mix between the muffin cases and
    sprinkle each one with a little dark brown sugar to
    decorate. Place the muffins in the oven and bake for
    around 25 minutes, or until a skewer inserted into the
    middle of a muffin comes out clean. Place on a wire
    rack to cool.

Makes 12 muffins

260g / 9oz self-raising flour
1 tsp baking powder
1 tsp ground cinnamon
115g / 4oz light brown sugar
2 eggs
120ml / ½ cup oat milk or other
  milk of your choice
4 tbsp sunflower oil
120g / 4oz sultanas
170g / 6oz grated apple
2 tbsp dark brown sugar

Use what you've grown
You can use any eating or cooking apples for this recipe. If using
cookers, you may want to add a little more sugar.

Rhubarb crumble muffins

I don't think I know many people who don't appreciate a good rhubarb crumble, so to alter this classic pudding to make lovely fruity muffins in the spring / early summer seemed like a good plan, and it was definitely an all-round success. Rhubarb makes a lovely, moist muffin, and the crumble topping adds a nice, crunchy contrast.

1. Heat the oven to 190°C / 375°F fan, and line a muffin tin with 12 paper cases. Stir the sugar and rhubarb together in a large bowl and set aside.

2. Make up the crumble topping by combining the sugar, flour, oats and allspice together in a bowl, then rub the butter in with your fingertips until lumpy but well mixed.

3. Stir the oil, egg, vanilla, oat milk and cider vinegar into the bowl, with the rhubarb. In a separate bowl combine the flour, baking powder and bicarbonate of soda, then add the dry ingredients to the wet and mix well.

Makes 12 muffins

For the muffins
170g / 6oz caster sugar
170g / 6oz rhubarb, halved
   lengthways then diced
2 tbsp sunflower oil
1 egg
1 tsp vanilla extract
120ml / ½ cup oat milk or nut
   milk of your choice
1 tsp cider vinegar
225g / 8oz plain flour
1 tsp baking powder
1 tsp bicarbonate of soda

Continued on next page

4. Quickly spoon the mixture into the muffin cases and top each one with the crumble, then bake in the oven for 18–20 minutes, or until a skewer inserted into the centre of a muffin comes out clean. Remove from the oven and place on a wire rack to cool.

For the crumble topping
60g / 2oz soft dark brown sugar
60g / 2oz plain flour
30g / 1oz porridge oats
1 tsp ground allspice
60g / 2oz butter

Vegan and gluten-free rhubarb crumble muffins

We have lots of people coming to courses at Homeacres who have different dietary requirements, and I always do my best to provide alternatives or make sure that most of the recipes that day are edible for them. I don't want anyone to ever miss out on the fantastic flavours of Charles's amazing produce. I make these in a big batch and then pop them in the freezer so we can get one or two out when needed. When we've had more than a couple of people who are vegan and gluten-free, I have made these for the whole group, and so many people have been surprised that without dairy and wheat flour, muffins can still taste so good.

1. Heat the oven to 190°C / 375°F fan, and line a muffin tin with 12 paper cases. Stir the sugar and rhubarb together in a large bowl and set aside.

2. Make up the crumble topping by mixing the sugar, buckwheat flour, oats and allspice together in a bowl, and then rub the coconut oil in with your fingertips until lumpy.

3. Stir the rosewater, oil, oat milk and cider vinegar into the bowl, with the rhubarb. In a separate bowl combine the flour, baking powder and bicarbonate of soda, then add the dry ingredients to the wet and mix well.

4. Quickly spoon the mixture into the muffin cases and top with the crumble, then bake in the oven for 18–20 minutes, or until a small skewer inserted into the centre of a muffin comes out clean. Remove from the oven and place on a wire rack to cool.

Makes 12 muffins

For the muffins
170g / 6oz rhubarb, sliced
  lengthways then diced
170g / 6oz sugar
260g / 9oz buckwheat flour
½ tsp baking powder
1 tsp bicarbonate of soda
1 tsp cider vinegar
1 tbsp rose water
120ml / ½ cup vegetable oil
120ml / ½ cup oat milk or nut
  milk of your choice

For the crumble topping
60g / 2oz soft dark brown sugar
60g / 2oz buckwheat flour
30g / 1oz porridge oats
1 tsp ground allspice
60g / 2oz coconut oil

Charles's advice on growing your own

Carrot

The flavour of homegrown carrots is just so different! A man on one of my courses said it was carrots that got him keen to grow vegetables, after he had sown a few seeds in a pot of compost outside the kitchen door. He had never grown any vegetables before, and when he pulled the first carrot to eat he was simply amazed at how it tasted.

I suspect that a majority of the population no longer has any inkling about the taste and sweetness of properly grown carrots, or many other vegetables. They are missing it, and do not know they are missing it!

Be patient before you sow. Carrots were the first seeds I ever sowed, in January 1981. The seed packet said you could sow from January outside, and who was I to disbelieve the 'experts'? I didn't harvest a carrot from that sowing in 1981, in fact I never saw any leaves either.

Two sowings in a year can cover most of your needs.

- Make your first sowing in early spring, which here is from mid-March. They will harvest through summer.
- Sow carrots in early summer, to harvest through autumn and store in winter.

Yields vary according to variety and time of year; can be up to 6 kg / m².

Even in the warmth of summer, homegrown carrots can store for up to a month. Just leave any soil or compost on them after pulling, and keep in a paper sack somewhere cool. Storing carrots for winter is the same process, and they do not need to be packed in sand.

Courgette

The flavour and texture of courgettes are best when fresh, so this is a huge advantage for homegrown. The flowers are also delicious to eat, for example fried after being dipped in a little batter.

However, plants grow large, and in small gardens they may not be practical because of their need for space. There is an option with varieties like Black Forest to grow them up strings. Also there are summer squash varieties of varied colour, shape and texture. All are nicest to eat when young, with soft skins and the seeds not yet developed.

They are warmth-loving: sow from mid-spring, after checking
your last frost date. Sow no more than three weeks before last frost,
under cover.

Harvests are continuous through summer and until first frost.
The yield is higher if you let them grow large before picking.

Courgettes are mostly water and have soft skins, so they don't store
for long. You can keep them for a week in the fridge or maybe three days
at ambient temperature, after which they turn soft and rubbery.

Index

Acknowledgements

Catherine

Firstly, I would like to thank you, Charles, for introducing me to no dig and letting me into your world at Homeacres. For me, it is a spiritual place that nourishes my soul, and it is such a privilege to work with you. Thank you too for giving me the opportunity to share my recipes with the world. You have been enthusiastic and supportive from the very beginning and I hope I have done your faith justice.

Thanks to Mum and Dad (Shirley and Ron) for feeding me so well when I was growing up and always being so supportive. You are both a constant source of inspiration in growing and cooking. Special thanks go to Mum for helping me in the kitchen at Homeacres when I was just too pregnant to do it alone, and for testing so many recipes for me. I literally could not have done it without you. To Nathan for your constant encouragement and unwavering support to take on this project while I grew our baby. I wasn't sure I could do it, but you always were. And for all those who helped along the way, Helen Frances Claire Parnham for coaching me to start this, Myfanwy Milward for your knowledge and expertise throughout, and all of those who tested recipes and gave me your feedback. Thank you.

Charles

The idea for this cookbook originated with Kate Forrester, who was creating lovely meals for the courses at Homeacres until she moved on to start her own market garden. Catherine then took over and made delicious meals for us all, and has now assembled this selection of wonderful recipes. Thanks to James Pople for his many ideas and photographs. He then laid out this beautiful book, and kept us on track in the process. Course days at Homeacres are hectic by lunchtime, as the food piles up and hungry participants come into the conservatory. Thanks to Briony Plant for helping with photography at that point.